D0495064

MICHAEL PARKINSON
ON GOLF

MICHAEL PARKINSON

ON GOLF

Michael Parkinson

Illustrated by John Ireland

Hodder & Stoughton

Copyright © 1999 by Michael Parkinson

First published in Great Britain in 1999
by Hodder and Stoughton
A division of Hodder Headline PLC

The right of Michael Parkinson to be identified as the Author of
the Work has been asserted by him in accordance with the
Copyright, Designs and Patents Act 1988.

10 9 8 7

All rights reserved. No part of this publication may be
reproduced, stored in a retrieval system, or transmitted,
in any form or by any means without the prior written
permission of the publisher, nor be otherwise circulated
in any form of binding or cover other than that in which
it is published and without a similar condition being
imposed on the subsequent purchaser.

British Library Cataloguing in Publication Data

A CIP catalogue record for this title
is available from the British Library

ISBN 0 340 75183 5

Typeset by Hewer Text Ltd, Edinburgh
Printed and bound in Great Britain by
Mackays of Chatham, plc.

Hodder and Stoughton
A division of Hodder Headline PLC
338 Euston Road
London NW1 3BH

CONTENTS

Michael Parkinson on Golf

Confessions of an Amateur

CONTENTS

CAPTAIN'S DAY HORRORS

INTRODUCTION

On the day of the solar eclipse I played golf. As the earth slipped into the shadow of the moon I made par on the fifth at Temple Golf Club. Thus one cosmic event was celebrated by another.

Historians eager for the minutiae of totality should know I hit a seven iron which finished six feet from the pin. I missed the birdie putt because the light was by then olive green and in any case I didn't want to upstage the main event.

After that I couldn't hit my backside with the proverbial banjo. I must have looked at the sun or it could have been eclipse sickness. More likely it was all part of the eternal struggle between those people who design golf courses and the rest of mankind.

The account of my place in that struggle forms the greater part of this book. As I point out in later chapters the fascination with golf is that it defines the difference between man's aspirations and his achievements. There is much humour in it. To enjoy it to its limits it is as necessary to laugh at one's self as it is to cultivate a good swing.

This book is dedicated to all those golfers who fall short of their golfing ambitions but never stop laughing at their folly. In particular it is for Mary Parkinson, who introduced me to the game; Laurie Holloway, who taught me its rhythms and its etiquette; and my sons in the hope they develop better swings than their father.

I'd like to mention a couple of golf courses too. Temple in the Thames Valley, where the cover photograph was shot, is as pretty and as pleasant a members' club as you will find and Wentworth is as challenging as they come. I am a member and servant of both.

Most of the chapters in the book originally appeared as articles in the *Daily Telegraph*. My thanks to David Welch and Nigel Seymour for their encouragement and for laughing in the right places.

Summer Games

I AM a summer man myself. I was put on earth to stand in shafts of sunlight. That I have lived all my life in a mostly grey, damp and chilly land only goes to prove that you can't win 'em all.

Ideally, I would have loved to have been one of those beach Lotharios you see in the South of France and other temples of sybaritic pleasures. I would speak English with an amazing French accent, be adept at all water sports, lithe of limb, teak brown and fill my bikini briefs.

Any killjoy who might point out that this was not a pensionable occupation should know that I have already seen the perfect job for my retirement. It is at premises held by a middle-aged beach dweller in Queensland, Australia who whiles away his days spraying suntan oil on to scantily clad young ladies. Fun without ruin. Also I have chosen his job, rather than other similar occupations on beaches in other lands, because it is my experience that Australian beach beauties give you more to spray at.

I am ill-prepared for such a job. The beaches of my youth were places you stared at from the haven of an adjacent bus shelter. Frustration being the mother of invention, we turned the shelter into a cricket pavilion and the windswept beach into Lord's. Thus we conceived the game of beach cricket, a means of using the facilities to hand while reducing the danger of death from exposure.

The driving force behind the enterprise was my late father, to whom cricket was not so much a way of life, more a religious experience. When he died I offered the thought that if they didn't play cricket in heaven he would ask for a transfer and I wasn't being clever.

Being a Yorkshireman, he had no time for any game of cricket that did not resemble a full-scale war. He therefore insisted that our opponents should consist of teams of holidaying Lancastrians so that we might fight the War of the Roses on Bridlington sands. He would roam the boarding houses and amusement arcades listening for the peculiar accents of those who live on the wrong side of the Pennines. When he had identified the enemy, he would make the offer they could not refuse, which consisted of enquiring whether or not they fancied being thrashed by a team of Yorkshiremen.

For ten seasons or more we played beach cricket and never once lost a game. This had little to do with the strength of our team but was almost entirely brought about by my father's unique grasp of the tactics peculiar to the game he invented.

Every morning before a big game he would spend some

time studying the tidal reports. This would have a profound effect upon the result because the boundaries of our game were the harbour wall and the sea. Thus, when the tide was about a mile out he would ask the opposing team to bat first, knowing that they had no chance of reaching the sea boundary and would likely be knackered at the end of their innings, having had to run for everything.

He would delay the commencement of our knock until the tide had turned and the sea was within a reasonable distance. Then he would instruct our batsmen to take no chances until they observed the opposing fielders standing knee deep in water. The tactic was to hoist the ball over their heads into the North Sea, when retrieving it became a test of nerve and character. On one occasion deep square leg was so far out to sea he was treading water and on another an opponent who swam like a dolphin was heading towards the coast of Norway in pursuit of a big hit when he was intercepted by the lifeboat from Flamborough Head.

In the end, we were defeated by a combination of despair and affluence. Fed-up with being thrashed, the Lancastrians sought refuge on the Costa del Sol. The old man followed them but when he discovered that the Mediterranean was non-tidal he retired to write the definitive volume on the tactics of the game he invented. The rest of his team went their different ways.

I tried beach cricket in the Caribbean, which made me thankful that there had not been too many Jamaicans taking their holidays in Bridlington when I was a lad. In the West Indies beach cricket is not an alternative to the real thing; it is a training ground for the international arena. There are several members of the present West Indian cricket team who prepared their careers by bowling at me on Caribbean beaches. Anyway, that's my story and I'm sticking to it, if only to explain why I played several games out there and can honestly say I never saw a ball that was bowled at me.

It was this traumatic experience as much as anything that led me into golf's seductive embrace. I had retired hurt from my latest (and last) game of beach cricket and was attempting to get my bruises sunburned when the wife suggested I spend my sunlit days in pursuit of a less dangerous ambition.

I found a partner at the local golf club and embarked on my new venture. It had looked such a simple game I couldn't understand why I was so inept at it.

Nor did it help that my partner, a man well into his seventies who looked as if he might need a walking frame, knocked the ball about with easy nonchalance. He was polite and solicitous about my plight, until at the tenth hole I drove my ball into a snake-infested jungle and said, 'Who on earth built this bloody golf course?'

'As a matter of fact, I did,' he said.

This is how I came to form the Anti-Golf Society. This organisation prospered for a while, particularly in Spain where I recruited several frustrated wives who didn't realise until too late that the Costa del Sol is the name of a golf course stretching from Malaga airport to Gibraltar. Our most effective moment occurred in Marbella when we organised a competition for the Worst Golfing Experience of the Week, to find the person who played the round that made him wish he had never taken up golf. It was won by a gentleman from Glamorgan who went round in 120 – including a spectacular 15 on a par three where he had some trouble with a bunker – and threw his golf bag into a nearby lake, not realising he had put his car keys and traveller's cheques in one of the pockets. He slipped a disc while trying to retrieve it and when he got back to the hotel discovered his girlfriend (made wanton by his absence and too much sangria) in a romantic dalliance with a Spanish crimper. Needless to say, he did not turn up to receive his prize, being under heavy sedation in a darkened room, safe from the game that had proved to be his undoing.

Unwisely, I disbanded the Anti-Golf Society a few years ago and became a fan of the game. This conversion was entirely pragmatic. With maturity comes the realisation that most ambitions are fantasies. I am never going to be a beach Adonis. Let someone else spray girls with oil on that beach in Queensland. If I am going to spend my declining years standing in pools of sunlight, then I haven't got the time for sitting in bus shelters waiting for a fine day in Cleethorpes.

Nowadays, whenever the sun shines I am off in pursuit, golf bag on my shoulder, poacher turned gamekeeper but totally unrepentant. The joy of golf is that even when the sun goes behind a cloud there is always a laugh to be had.

I was recently playing with my good friend Mr James

Tarbuck whose fanaticism about the game I can only liken to my father's attitude towards cricket. He was standing over a putt on the last hole of a course in Surrey where a public footpath runs close to the green. There was money on the shot and at such a moment Mr Tarbuck is not to be messed with. He had carefully and painstakingly lined up and had drawn the putter back when a citizen approached.

'Excuse me,' he said. Mr Tarbuck looked up in disbelief. 'Can you tell me how I get to the cemetery?' he enquired.

'Try dying,' said Mr Tarbuck, affably enough.

August 1988

TALKING TO HEROES AND PROS

Man Who Inhabited a Barren Landscape and Made it Flower

I HAVE a new four wood I am dying to use. Then I look out of the window. The river has invaded the lower reaches of the garden and the low cloud sits on top of the bare branches opposite. It's like being in a seeping tunnel. If I were a hardy golfer, I'd be out and about, but the older I get the less inclined I am to dress for golf as if for a polar expedition.

It is sad to think that unless I go in pursuit of the sun the likelihood is I will not play golf for another three months, but it's salutary to contemplate the advice the great Walter Hagen gave to golfers. He said: 'Don't hurry. Don't worry. You're only here on a short visit, so don't forget to stop and smell the roses.' Not only did Mr Hagen practise what he preached, but he ordered that the words be inscribed on his coffin when he died.

Walter Hagen's philosophy has always struck me as being one of the most attractive, as well as profound, observations made about the game of golf. No doubt some of today's grit and grimace brigade would dismiss Hagen's doctrine as being totally unsuitable for the present time when the stakes are so high and the pressure (that awful word) so extreme. That being the case they should understand that the present financial bonanza in golf is due almost entirely to Walter Hagen, that he was the man who established the humble golf pro as highly paid star and that when it comes to pressure the modern golfer doesn't know what he is talking about. The real pressure was on men like Hagen who inhabited a barren landscape and made it flower. All the modern pro has to do is turn up.

When Hagen started his career, the possibility of earning a million dollars from the game was unthinkable. Hagen did it. It took him a lifetime's work during which he won eleven British and American major titles. However, his fortune did not come from prize money. The prize for winning the British Open in the 1920s was $300. Hagen used to give the money to his caddie.

Hagen made real money from exhibition games, gambling and having the clever idea sixty years ago that there might be a future building golf courses in Florida.

Today's pro golfers should have a whip-round and erect a shrine to the memory of Walter Hagen. I have always found him one of the most fascinating figures in sport. He won the British Open four times, in 1922, 1924, 1928 and 1929; the US Open twice, in 1914 and 1919; and between 1921 and 1927 won the American PGA Championship five times.

This is all the more remarkable when you consider it

was achieved by a man who chain-smoked, drank a lot of whiskey and was never known to refuse a party. After winning the Canadian Open he wired ahead to his hotel: 'Fill one bathtub of champagne.'

On the last day of the PGA Championship, when Hagen was due to play Leo Diegel for what was then the highest prize in professional golf, he arrived at the course wearing a dinner jacket after a night on the town. He was seen by a fan who said: 'Do you know that Diegel has been in bed since ten o'clock last night?'

'He might have been in bed,' said Hagen, 'but he wasn't sleeping.' He beat Diegel 5 and 3.

Hagen's real importance to golf was that by the force of his own remarkable personality and his innate belief that Jack was as good as his master (if not a darned sight better) he changed attitudes towards professionals. He made them respectable and gave them esteem. Even

today his disregard for convention would ruffle a few feathers.

For instance, it was rumoured that he said to the Duke of Windsor during a round of golf: 'Hold the pin, Eddie'. Hagen denied the story.

'What I said was, "Hold the pin, Caddie," he said. He was once due to play a round of golf with a prince of Japan. He arrived late.

'The prince has waited two hours for you,' he was told.

'Well?' said Hagen. 'He wasn't going anywhere, was he?'

He wore beautiful suits, drank champagne and drove fast cars. He employed a glamorous blonde secretary who played the ukulele. He lived in style and expected to be treated like a star. If he arrived at a venue and thought the amenities inadequate he would decline to play until they were improved. He refused to be treated like a second-class citizen and by doing so made things better for all his tribe.

He was an intriguing mixture: a showman and a revolutionary, a dandy and a radical. It is always fruitless to speculate what the great players of yesteryear would be worth in the modern game, but there is little doubt that Hagen, with his genius for golf and for living, would be top of any list.

He would be delighted with the money in the game, but what, I wonder, would he make of the grim and remorseless grind that modern golf has become? Not much time to stop and smell the roses.

December 1992

Single Mind That Created the Champion of Millions

THE schoolboys were twittering with excitement at the arrival of the world's greatest golfer. Nick Faldo selected a wedge, loosened up with a few purposeful swings, and then said: 'If you boys will tell me your golfing problems, then I'll try and show you what to do.'

A small child raised his hand. 'What's your problem?' asked Nick.

'Please, sir, I only have one arm,' said the boy. The golfer didn't blink.

'I can hit a ball with one hand. Let's have a competition,' he said.

The boy, frail and nervous as a chick, set up. His swing was rushed and excitable. Faldo re-aligned him, showed him how to turn so he had a steeper swing. The boy swung again and hit the ball further than he had ever done before. Master and pupil beamed in satisfaction.

For more than an hour, in drenching rain, he taught and demonstrated. It was the best golf lesson they will ever have. Moreover, it was free. Faldo showed great charm and patience with the children.

In that respect he was like two other great athletes I have observed at close quarters – Boycott and Best – both of whom, like Faldo, have often been at conflict with the adult world. Their rapport with youngsters has something to do with the uncluttered enthusiasm of children, their genuine acceptance of heroes. Adults make preconceived judgments about people, children take as they find.

Nick Faldo drew the driver from his bag, unsheathing it in dramatic fashion as if revealing a magic sword. The children gibbered with excitement. He boomed a drive across the practice ground and over a hedge.

'That's in the swimming pool, sir,' said a boy, hopping with delight. Another majestic drive disappeared from sight. 'That's the greenhouse,' the boys squealed!

'Any requests?' he said.

'Can you hit the clock on the pavilion, sir?' was one.

'Better not, but I'll hit a low one, just over it,' he said. The ball screamed a yard or two over the clock, as nominated. By this time, the boys were almost wetting themselves with joy.

'Heroes are important, aren't they?' said Nick Faldo later. 'If you're lucky, they inspire you. Mine were Nicklaus and Palmer. When I was young, I'd play imaginary games against them. I'd take four balls out. There'd be Jack, Arnie, Tom Weiskopf and me. I'd play their shots, try to emulate their swings. I'd imagine features on the course at Welwyn that weren't there, like lakes and extra bunkers.

'I'd start at eight o'clock in the morning and play until dark. Thirty-six holes and then I'd practise. Sometimes, I'd play a hole backwards. In other words, if it was a three-wood, five-iron to the green, I'd take a five-iron off the tee and a three-wood to the green.

'They sent me on a scholarship to college in America. It's the kind of situation young golfers dream about. But it wasn't for me. Studies got in the way of golf. Also, they reckoned they worked us hard, but I was working four times as hard on my own at Welwyn. I just walked away from it.

'I was good at most games but as soon as I picked up a golf club at fourteen, I knew this was the game for me.

'I didn't like team games, so I tried swimming but that bored me. Swimming up and down the baths all day long until you were blue and wrinkled wasn't for me. Then I got into cycling but that was boring, too. A good practice was if you fell off your bike exhausted and puked. Again, not for me. The difference with golf is imagination. That's the reason I'm never bored when I practise. It's such a complex and difficult game but it's also artistic.

'I remember the first time I heard someone say, "He played a shot punched low under the wind." It stirred my imagination. I couldn't wait to get out on the practice range and interpret what I thought it meant.

'It's the reason I prefer fly fishing to ordinary fishing. The idea of chucking a line into murky water, and sitting and hoping, doesn't appeal. But the joy of casting in clear waters, where you can see the trout and the bugger can see you, is wonderful because it's a great skill and a marvellous contest.'

Nick Faldo is the archetypal working-class hero, the man who demonstrated that by hard work and dedication you could take on the world and be the best. He is tall, fit and strong, with boyish good looks, size eleven feet and beautiful hands.

He knows he is the best golfer in the world but he is no braggart; he has more money than he can spend but he is not flash about it. So why is it that he is not beloved like Frank Bruno, or Gary Lineker, or Sandy Lyle, even? Is it that we are uncomfortable with true greatness? Are we perhaps misinformed by mischievous elements in the media who, for one reason or another, have it in for the likes of Nick Faldo?

He says: 'I don't understand what they say. First, I'm a loner. Well, if that means that I don't go into a bar at the end of the day and have a few drinks, then I suppose I am. But I don't see that makes me a bad person. I've always

preferred to concentrate on my game. When I'm at a tournament, I'm at work, I don't drink at work. It's as simple as that.

'Then they say I'm a miserable bugger. I like to be focused, to concentrate. I find it difficult to smile and joke like some do. Let's imagine I've just shot six birdies on the trot and, at the seventh hole, I laugh and joke with the gallery and then make a bogey. I wouldn't know if it was because I'd mucked about with the spectators. So I try to eliminate all the risks.

'Also, I'm shy. I do find it difficult to relate to the spectators sometimes, because if I start chatting them up some might think I'm a big-headed sod who's showing off.

'They say I'm not like Seve. But, then, who is, and why should I be? He hits the ball into the trees on three consecutive holes and keeps on scoring, but that's the way he is. If I hit three balls into the trees, I'd give the game up. He has this happy-go-lucky reputation. But I'll tell you what, he doesn't look that happy coming down the eighteenth when he's scored 74. Who would? But they don't mention that, do they?

'Then they accuse me of being "Mechanical Man". This really gets my goat. Makes me sound like a battery toy. What my game is about is control. It's the ability to shape the ball at will, to make it behave just as I want it to. What's mechanical about that?

'The conclusion is that these people don't really want to know me. If they can't be bothered to take one step closer, to see the real person, then sod 'em.'

To expect Faldo to take a more measured, philosophical approach to his detractors would be to misunderstand the man and what makes him tick. He works harder than anyone he knows at getting things right. He leaves little to chance and genuinely cannot understand people who appear not to comprehend what he is striving for. It's not just mere mortals, either. He has been known to walk down a fairway, head tipped to heaven, addressing the Almighty: 'Dear God, how much harder do you want me to work to get it right?' is what he says.

Only a zealot could have decided, as Faldo did in 1985, to change his swing. It was as if Geoffrey Boycott decided in mid-career to bat left-handed, or Lester Piggot to make his come-back riding side-saddle. Faldo was already recognised as a world-class player but it obviously was not good enough. The demons inside him urged him to try for something else. What was it? 'Perfection,' I suggested.

'No such thing,' said Nick Faldo. 'What I was after, and still am, is control. I want to be in total charge of my game, hit, fade or draw, just as I visualise the shot. It was the right ambition, but it nearly brought me down. Those were the black days. I was very depressed. The mistake I made was in trying to play tournament golf while re-structuring the swing.

'I didn't play well and they started writing me off. "We've seen the best of him," seemed to be the general tone.

'I'd arrive at an airport and I'd see some of the other pros waiting for their baggage and they'd be demonstrating my new swing or the exercises I had to do. They'd shake their heads as if they thought I'd gone mad.

'Everyone assumes that when I went to Lead [David Leadbetter, Faldo's coach that time] in search of a new swing, we had already designed one. Not true. It was an uncharted journey for both of us. I was a guinea pig.

'I'd hit fifteen hundred golf balls a day. I'd have to go for a swim halfway through in an attempt to relax my body. My fingers were so sore that they swelled up and I couldn't grip the club properly. I'd come home and find dinner ready, and I'd sneak out because I would have a thought about what I was doing wrong. When I got back, dinner was ruined.'

Some sponsors lost faith and cancelled contracts. Nick Faldo knows where they live. The company providing his sweaters gave him a new contract. Nick Faldo will not forget the gesture. It was an unpleasant but important part of his young life.

'At least, at the end of it, I knew who my friends were,' he said.

Apart from the expert help he received, there was friendly advice from the public. One letter, for example read: 'Dear Mr Faldo, I am a 16 handicap golfer but I am regarded as the best putter in my club and maybe I could give you a few tips.' Faldo laughs at the recollection and says: 'Mind you, you sometimes wonder if they might be right.'

One day in 1987 he went to Hattiesburg in America and shot four 67s.

'Everything fell into place,' he said. 'It was like sunshine.' It was a rebirth. In Britain the same year he won the first of his three Opens, and in '89 the US Masters for the first time. He wants two more titles to complete the set. And now?

'I still have the desire to hit a golf ball and to win. I look forward to many more years at the very top. After that, who knows?

'I suppose that in the end I would just like people to say, "I saw that Faldo play and, by God, he was a good golfer." ' Whatever else they might say about Nick Faldo, that much is guaranteed.

May 1988

Nick Faldo won his third Masters title in 1996 in heroic style after an unforgettable head to head with Greg Norman. Since then, nothing has gone right for Faldo. He had a well-publicised and acrimonious split with his coach, David Leadbetter, and seems quite unable to recapture the consistency that made him the world number one golfer. He now struggles to make the cut and has dropped out of the top one hundred golfers list. He is, however, too good a golfer and too determined a character to be written off.

Captain Gallacher Parades his Qualities of Leadership

BERNARD GALLACHER reminds me of a physical training instructor I met in the Army. This man made you feel scruffy just looking at him. Everything about him shone, from his burnished cap badge to his shiny black pumps. You could see your face in his pumps and I often did when he gave me twenty press-ups.

Bernard Gallacher is, I suspect, the sort of man who polishes the soles of his golf shoes, the soldier who looks

forward to kit inspections. He is one of those fortunate and blessed individuals who never looks crumpled.

When he was captain of the European Ryder Cup team, he stood before the scrutiny of journalists and cameras and announced the names of the golfers who would face America. The only twitch in his composure came when he announced Haeggman as one of his wild-card choices. As he did so, he twiddled the papers in his hand. He didn't know what to expect. What he got was a round of applause and from that moment on he was never again in danger of breaking sweat.

Ninety minutes later he was still answering questions with patience and humour. An exemplary figurehead. That done he moved into the next room to present prizes to the members of Wentworth Golf Club who knew him as their professional. It was a reminder to Bernard Gallacher that on the same day as the world's press hung on his every word he could still be given the golf shoes of a Wentworth member and asked to re-stud them. It would bring anyone down to earth, not that Bernard Gallacher is ever likely to lose touch with reality.

He was born in 1949 in the mining community of Bathgate. The course where he learnt to play golf near Edinburgh was situated between a railway line and a factory. His father and uncles were keen golfers and he was never in danger of becoming anything other than a golf pro. He turned professional at the age of nineteen and immediately became Rookie of the Year.

The next year he was the leading money-winner and from then until 1984 never fell below thirtieth on the money-list, seven times being placed ninth or better. He played his first Ryder Cup in 1969 and thereafter was a member of eight consecutive teams. In that time he played thirty-one games, won thirteen, lost thirteen and halved five. In 1976 he became the club professional at Wentworth. We talked in the garden of his home near Wentworth. I asked him if there was ever a problem readjusting from being captain of the Ryder Cup team to club professional.

'But what I am is a club professional. That's what I started out to be. I'm proud of the fact. Even when I was playing the circuit full-time I always regarded myself as the pro at Wentworth. I never had a sponsor, just the club behind me. It's a good relationship. They could cope with me being Ryder Cup captain. One member rang Lesley, my wife, and said: "Tell Bernard he ought to pick Canizares, he's playing really well."

'Whatever success I had on the tour was due to the great support I've always had from the club and the members. The tour was much different in the seventies from now. In those days they simply told you there was a game in Germany or France and you made your own way there.

'My education was travelling around Europe with a suitcase and a golf bag when sometimes even the local taxi driver didn't know where the golf course was. It made you self-sufficient, durable.

'Nowadays, the players have travel agents, sleep at first-class hotels, one or two have private planes and helicopters. They travel the world but see nothing. Very different. Another difference is you can get rich very quickly. You can also get finished very quickly, too. As I see it, the people at the top in golf are going to have much shorter careers and there are going to be many more casualties at the bottom,' he said.

He points out that there is possibly only Sam Torrance of the current players on the European Tour who shares his memory of what it was like before the gravy train arrived. It gives Gallacher a clear view of the way modern golf is going and the threat to its treasured traditions.

In his book about the 1991 Ryder Cup at Kiawah Island, Gallacher contrasts the start of the competition with what it has become. When Samuel Ryder and Walter Hagen took tea at Wentworth in 1926 to discuss the possibility of British and American professionals playing against each other on a two-yearly basis, they could never have imagined that their idea of a friendly get-together would grow into the multi-million dollar monster it is today.

Nor would they have approved of the shenanigans at Kiawah, when in the aftermath of the Gulf War the American team wore military-style forage caps much favoured by Stormin' Norman (General Schwarzkopf, American commander in the Gulf War), and one message of encouragement to the Americans exhorted them to 'kick butt'. It was a strange baptism for a purist like Gallacher.

He knew something was fundamentally amiss when, at the official dinner welcoming the two teams, the chief executive of the American PGA said grace and took the opportunity at the same time to pray aloud for an American win.

Gallacher said, 'Dave Stockton [the American captain] upped the temperature. He did so because he thought our supporters were more supportive and vociferous than theirs. I found the military forage caps distasteful, as I did Azinger's statement that they had beaten the Iraquis and were about to do the same to the Europeans.

'When I met Dan Quayle, the Vice President, I told him this had nothing to do with golf and it was an insult to the Europeans who had fought and died in the Gulf. It affected their spectators. I've never heard golfers being chanted on to the greens before.

'Then I got a phone call from a local disc jockey in the early hours of the morning. He said it was a "wake-up the enemy" call. Nick got one, so did one or two of the other players.

'I was proud of our team, they didn't respond. I was proud of myself, I said nothing. But I don't think there will be a repeat. Tom Watson stood on the sidelines at Kiawah and saw what was going on and I don't think he approved of what he saw.

'What I want our spectators to do is behave exactly as they do at a British Open. I don't want barracking on the greens or people making a noise on a player's back-swing.

'So far golf has been free from the kind of crowd behaviour we get at soccer – and sometimes cricket – matches. I hope it continues to set the example because if it doesn't that will be the end of the Ryder Cup and that would be a great pity,' said Gallacher.

Was he confident in his team? 'Very. I never had any doubt about picking Seve. I'm afraid he was under added pressure to play well but he carries that sort of pressure with him. He's never let alone and maybe that's a reason why he found it difficult to regain form,' he said.

Might it be that Ballesteros will never be the same player again? Put most cruelly, is he past it?

'I don't think so. I suppose something has got to give, even in a genius like Seve, but I think that under certain circumstances he will still win majors. He has got to work things out for himself. The trouble is he's offered advice from all quarters. There such an overwhelming desire for him to come good.

'But in all the speculation about Seve let me tell you that he's still the one the Americans fear, the one they most want to beat. He was the first European to start winning in the States.

'He would play in Europe, nip over to America and win a big one, come back home, play some more then nip off again to America and win again. They didn't like it. But he broke the mould, showed the others it could be done. If Nick, Langer, Woosie and Sandy owe anybody anything, they owe something to Seve. He was the one who showed them the way in America.

'Although we lost in Kiawah I was very heartened by what happened there. The last hour of play revealed a lot about the quality of my team. When Langer missed that putt it didn't really matter because we had done our best and that was the important thing.

'What I said at the time was that I didn't think that in future any player, either European or American, should have the awful responsibility of a putt on the last green to decide the match. It should be settled before that.

'It was fortunate, in a sense, that it was Bernhard who had the putt. He's the strongest, most resilient of players. It could have destroyed a younger, less purposeful man, ruined his career. As it was, Bernhard went out very next tournament and won it. What a man. But I still wouldn't want anyone to face what he did again.'

But it could happen, so what would he suggest? He thought for a moment and said: 'If at The Belfry the Americans had a two-foot putt to tie on the last hole, I hope I'd have had the guts to walk onto the green and give it to them.'

September 1993

Visitors to Bernard Gallacher's beloved Wentworth are confronted nowadays by a lifesized bronze statue of himself. The Wentworth Club further honoured him by selecting him as their Millennium Captain.

Norman Strikes Out to Escape Twilight Zone

FIRST of all he doesn't look like a Great White Shark. Anthropomorphically speaking, he is more a bird of prey than a fish, his features aquiline, his pale eyes slightly hooded. In a straight comparison with the rest of the human race, Greg Norman would come in that special category manufactured by the Lord on one of his better days.

He is perfectly equipped to be a modern sporting hero. He looks the part: broad-shouldered, slim-hipped, good legs. He has the appearance of a contender for the light heavyweight title. In a game sometimes dulled by a grim pursuit of perfection, he is a glorious individual, striking the ball a country mile in an exciting charge for the spoils. He is an idol pursued by doting fans; a bankable commodity sought by advertisers and sponsors who want to stuff his pockets full of dollars; a superstar lionised by captains of industry, showbiz glitterati, prime ministers, presidents and kings.

He owns a jet worth £6 million, has a company building nineteen golf courses in Asia. He is a major shareholder in a firm manufacturing golf clubs with sales of £15 million a year. He owns a boat, seven Ferraris and a Rolls-Royce. Without exerting himself unduly or over-taxing the imagination of those employed to extend his fortune, he can reckon on a basic income of £7 million each year. He has just been paid more than £300,000 for playing five rounds of golf in Australia. It is estimated his net income is £30–35 million.

Gregory John Norman is thirty-nine years old and on top of the world, yet still driven by the notion that it might all end tomorrow. He is still pursued by demons. In the past few years he has changed his swing, his coach, his caddie and his management team. Everything except his wife.

Observing him in Australia these past two weeks has been a fascinating and sometimes confusing study of a man coming face to face with the advisability of treading softly on native turf. In the public estimation, a convincing case could be made for Norman being the most respected and adored Australian sportsman since Don Bradman. The Australian media have always taken a more sceptical view.

Their caution seemed justified when Norman made a series of criticisms in Melbourne about the Australian Masters event he was playing in. In particular, his critics made much of his complaint that the prize-money of $750,000 compared unfavourably with purses in America. It was pointed out that in a country in recession with

high unemployment some might regard three-quarters of a million dollars as a lot of money for a game of golf. An even more hurtful observation was that the prize-money would be substantially more if Australia didn't have to cough up appearance money to players, like the £150,000 paid to Greg Norman.

The predicament his critics face is they know that in the absurd, not to say obscene, financial wheeler-dealing of golf, Norman is worth every penny, and that without his presence any major golf tournament in Australia would be struggling.

It is a dependency weighing heavily on both Greg Norman and his beloved Australia, and it is part of the turmoil within a man who, perhaps for the first time, has begun to feel confident enough to stand alone and say what he really feels.

His break with IMG may be the most significant manifestation of his state of mind. Together he and Mark McCormack's organisation were a formidable proposition in the world of golf. But when you are the best golfer in the world, do you need to be part of a stable?

We talked in Laguna Quays, Queensland (of which more later), near where he grew up. He occupied the Presidential Suite (what else?) of the hotel. From his window the Whitsunday Islands were hazy in the morning sun. The day before he had buzzed the hotel in his jet.

'My wake-up call,' he explained. 'Did I ever think I'd own an aeroplane? Jesus, I never thought I'd even own a house. I was an assistant pro earning the equivalent of fourteen pounds a week. They told me I'd never make it. I earned my fare to fly to Europe by gambling on a game of golf. It was a tough school. If you had a bad round on Friday you could be qualifying again on Monday. Taught you tenacious golf. Made you like a bull terrier. Nowadays young players are stroked like poodles, wined and dined.

'Mine was a tough school but I have to say I was lucky because I was put on earth at the right time in the right place with the right skills.

'I came into golf with the big money, not just from tournaments but the golf course design boom, people wanting to spend eight hundred million dollars on a monument to themselves. Even my setbacks have proved positive. At the lowest point of my career, in 1991, my wife said she thought I ought to give the game up for twelve months.

'I talked to myself in the mirror. It's something I do when I need to find out the truth, what I really feel. I said, "Do you want to give up golf?" And the mirror replied, "No, because I'll miss the competition." I said, "Do you really want it again? Are you prepared for all the hard work and the sacrifice?" And the answer was yes so I said let's go out and get it.

'Then I was in my car driving to practice and I pulled into the side of the road and watched the clouds. They were so peaceful. And I thought, "God, I want peace in my mind again." I decided then and there to get all the bullshit out of my brain. It worked. I just stared at the clouds and let all the good things come back into my mind. Within ninety days I had stopped worrying about what to do on a golf course and was concentrating on what I love to do which is play golf. I didn't seek out a sports psychologist. I think it's better to go through your problems alone.'

'When I was a child I was frightened of going into a darkened room. I used to reach my hand in first to switch on the lights. But I taught myself to enter the dark without putting the lights on. I conquered my fear. It's the same with playing golf.

'Larry Bird, the great basketball player, told me that with five seconds to go and his team losing by a point he *wanted* the ball. I thought that was interesting. Not hiding, no fear of failure. In the British Open at Sandwich on the last day I hit a nine-iron at the ninth to within two inches to go into a one-shot lead. And all the way in I kept reminding myself of what Larry had said. I *wanted* that one-shot lead.

'It is this mental approach to golf I've only just started learning about. I have a book called *Zen and the Martial Arts* which I read all the time and try to incorporate ways of relaxing and breathing into my golf game. I am going to see the champion kick-boxers in America because the way they relax their big muscles until the point of impact is very much what should happen when you are playing golf. None of this might work but I like a challenge.

'Mentally I am still learning about myself. What is important is to look at a 240 yard shot to the green over a lake, take the three-wood and be in the right frame of mind to succeed. Then you can say, "Boy, that was great because I *wanted* it!"

'I have written down at home a statement by President Roosevelt that he would rather experience the ecstasy of victory and the pain of defeat than spend any time in the grey twilight of life. That's what I feel. That's the way I want to play my golf,' he said.

His critics will tell you that Greg Norman is in danger of forgetting he is a golfer, that he is concentrating more on creating a business dynasty than winning Opens. It could still be he proves them wrong.

February 1994

Norman's greatest battle in the past couple of seasons has been with injury. He had a shoulder operation in 1998 and was nine months away from the game before returning in the 1999 Masters when he celebrated his comeback by finishing third. He remains one of the biggest attractions in world golf. His game might have suffered from lay-off and injury but his star quality is undiminished.

Davies Refreshingly Clear About Golfing 'Privilege'

IN THE sometimes neurotic and obsessive world of professional golf, where beta-blockers calm the palpitating heart, where God and Sigmund Freud are called upon to soothe the mental turmoil and coaches are witch doctors casting spells to ward off the yips, it is refreshing to come across a golfer with a healthy disregard for such taradiddle.

We may draw what conclusions we like from the fact that we are reporting on a woman. There will be those who will see it as a significant statement in the battle of the sexes, and others – I have in mind several male golfers of my acquaintance – who will use it as yet further proof that there are two different games, golf and the version played by the members of the ladies' section.

Laura Davies takes no part in such conjecture. What she knows is that all she has to do to face life at the top is keep reminding herself that playing golf sure beats working in a supermarket.

As she says, 'Playing golf for a living isn't a real job is it? It's a privilege. It's also well paid.' At the same time as she went to number one in the ratings she passed the million dollar mark in earnings.

I am grateful to Miss Davies. An hour in her company was music to my ears. It is reassuring in the often loony world of professional sport, where half-formed youths are transformed into half-baked adults – and worse – to find someone like Laura Davies, who is both a genuine star and seemingly untrammelled by success.

For instance, she arrived a little late for the interview at the Berkshire Golf Club, not because this was her due but because she had been lurking in the car park not daring to enter the building until she was sure that someone she knew was inside.

After the interview she began her preparation for rejoining the American tour not by consulting her coach – she doesn't have one – or hitting a thousand balls on a practice range, but by playing a friendly fourball; a fiver front and back nine and a tenner on the game.

As she teed up, our photographer asked her if she would mind the noise of a camera clicking at the top of her backswing. Certain male golfers of my acquaintance would swoon at the very thought. What Laura Davies said was 'Go for it.'

What I am trying to convey is that Laura Davies is a pleasant and uncomplicated individual. It shows in her face, her frank and clear eyes and is sustained by her conversation which is straightforward and unpretentious.

She is 5ft 10in tall, broad-shouldered, with big feet. I don't know what she weighs but, as my dear departed grandfather would say, she'd crush some grass.

She hits the ball a very long way. In fact, she has recorded one drive of more than 350 yards and one just short of that target. Both were wind assisted, but anyone who has seen her play knows that she is capable of starting most tournaments 16 under par because she can reach the majority of par fives in two.

She has brought excitement to women's professional golf. Wherever she appears people turn up to see her play.

When she stood on the first tee at the Berkshire, there was an audience of club staff and golfers standing around wondering just how far she would smite it on the par five opening hole. Can she really hit it as far as the men pros?

'I'm no Greg Norman,' she says. 'But one day I'd love to play him off the back tees just to see how my power game stood up under the kind of pressure the men play under.

'When I practise, I play off the back tees all the time. Length isn't a problem. On a 465 yard par four I can take a driver from the tee and then a three-iron to the green.

'That's what I do when I practise. What I'd like to see is if I could do it under the pressure of playing a men's tournament. Probably miss the cut, but I'd love the chance.'

She started playing golf when she was fourteen because her brother, Tony, took it up. Whatever Tony did, his sister imitated. She played football and cricket. Just before an event in America, she hurt her wrist playing cricket in a car park. She missed the cut.

As a child she envisaged a career as a sports teacher. As soon as she picked up a golf club she knew what she really wanted to do for the rest of her life. Her headmaster rebuked her ambition.

'You'll never earn a living playing golf,' he said. At sixteen she was playing for Surrey and already creating a stir with her big hitting. Playing in a final on the Old Course at Sunningdale, she reduced the opening par five to a drive and a nine-iron.

She was ready-made for an American sport scholarship. She declined. Why?

'Dunno really. Just wanted to stay at home.

'I played the amateur circuit for five years. Worked six months, played six months. I got jobs at a supermarket, a garage and a bookmakers before turning pro.

'My mum and step-dad were marvellous. Made a lot of

sacrifices. When I turned pro, I borrowed a thousand pounds from my parents. I missed the cut in the first tournament I played. Then I won four thousand pounds in the second. Since then I've never looked back.

'If any young players ask me what they should do to become a professional golfer, I tell them first of all to get a job so that when they come to play golf they'll understand it's a darned sight better than working. That's my philosophy.

'I had a couple of not so hot years in '91 and '92 and I started moaning and getting miserable. Then I just took stock and remembered what I was doing before I played golf every day.

'Since that time if I have a bad week I don't worry. It's an absolute privilege to be travelling the world playing golf. I think we have the best of the sporting world.

'Look at all the other champions in other sports like Nigel Mansell, who say they'd really rather be champion golfers. Ours is the best life. Look at how the men can go on earning money on the seniors tour,' she said.

I asked her if she thought there would be a seniors competition for women.

'Don't think so. Maybe the men will let us join theirs. That would be a way of playing with them. But most of the girls on the tour play until they're forty and then retire to have a family. Me? Another ten years I suppose. More if I'm still winning. Then I might think about packing up,' she said.

She has won twenty-seven tournaments worldwide. The question is, will the kind of success and fame we are talking about spoil Laura Davies? Will she be afflicted by the doubts and fears suffered by many of her male counterparts? Might she be tempted to employ a guru?

'I think that too much can be made of coaching. Look at Seve. I'm sure that if he got back to being Seve, when it was just him and his brother and there weren't all those people telling him what to do, things would be better.

'I'm lucky. I've never had a golf lesson in my life. I learned by mimicking others I saw play on the course or on the telly. I pick up more just watching the great players and copying them than I would from any teacher.

'You can't take your coach with you to Thailand can you? At least I can't. So if things go wrong I go to a range and start mucking about, getting the feel back. I'm more about feel than technique,' she said.

'What's feel?' I asked.

'Shaping the ball, drawing and fading it,' she said. Now this *is* highly technical. People have been trying to make the golf ball obey their command for hundreds of years. Books have been written on the subject, videos have been made, coaches have become rich by telling us how it's done. What is more, a multi-million dollar industry with space-age technology exists to design golf clubs to enable us better to master the game.

So come on, Laura Davies, what's this old baloney about feel?

'Well, if I stand over a shot and I think I've got to hit a draw, something happens to my swing and the ball goes right to left.

'If I want to hit a slice then I feel myself cut across the

ball as I hit. If I want to hit a draw or a slice or make the ball go low or high, I know what to do simply by having watched the great players on telly. I learned a lot watching Seve play, and Langer.

'What I learned from Bernhard was his rhythm with the irons. Woosie gave me a couple of tips for chipping, which came in useful. But the rest is what I've picked up just watching people. With me it's all about confidence. At present I'm confident and playing well. I feel I can't hit a bad shot,' she said.

The other good question to ask Laura Davies as she faces her glittering future is what about all that money waiting to be won? What will she do with it?

'Spend it,' she said. 'I love spending it. I've got three or four cars, bought a couple of cottages I've knocked into one next door to my mum. I don't worry too much about pensions.'

She loves a gamble. Indeed she confessed that as she passed Ascot racecourse on the way to our meeting she was tempted to pay a call. As it was, she settled for a bet.

Not only bookmakers have been on the receiving end of her generosity. She didn't mention it, but others told me that when Laura Davies won her first tournament she gave part of her winnings to the amateur organisation that had nurtured her.

She has helped out fellow pros who were struggling and has supported the European Tour without regard for the larger rewards that would come her way if she devoted all her time to playing in America.

When I asked her to name her greatest triumph, she

said being part of the team who won the Solheim Cup from the Americans.

When I asked her what she was most looking forward to in the future, she said defending the cup in America.

'Why?' I asked.

'Because it'll be great fun,' she said.

Interesting word, 'fun'. I think the reason I liked her so is because she can use the word and still convey the will to win that all great champions possess.

April 1994

Laura now has her own tournament. The Laura Davies International was inaugurated at Brocket Hall, Hertfordshire, in 1999. It is the first time a woman golfer has been given a tournament in Europe. She remains the brightest star in women's golf.

STRAIGHT FROM LAGUNA QUAYS TO JAWS OF HELL

C LEANING out the golf bag after returning from Australia was like looking at a scrapbook of our visit. I threw the sun block away, and the mosquito repellent. I also junked various sun hats and contemplated replacing them with a Balaclava. You think I jest. In fact, I am a great advocate of the Balaclava as an indispensable part of the wardrobe of a sporting gentleman.

In my younger days I sometimes wore a natty white Balaclava for the opening of the cricket season. These were knitted for me by me saintly mother who had a theory that her child would live longer if covered from head to toe in wool. She sometimes went too far, once knitting a cover for my cricket bat. I did not believe that my team-mates in the Barnsley dressing-room were ready for such a radical fashion statement and hid it at the bottom of my cricket bag.

Similarly, I am not too sure how a Balaclava would be

regarded by fellow members of Temple Golf Club. Might it be deemed unsuitable attire? I am taking no chance which is why my mother, still knitting after all these years, is now churning out woollen caps to keep my head warm. In fact, I am kept alive on the golf course by the concern of kindly gentlewomen. When I wrote of the problems I have gripping the club in cold weather because of poor circulation, I was sent a pair of sheepskin wrist cuffs by a woman who is similarly afflicted and who swears the cuffs do the trick. They made their debut at Temple the other day and will survive no sterner test.

We were a threeball. Our only chance of persuading a fourth player to accompany us would have been if Ranulph Fiennes lived in the area. There have been times when I have stood on the first tee at Temple Golf Club and been moved to sing a few verses of 'There'll Always Be An England'. These are the days when the sun glints on the distant Thames as it meanders through Marlow, the distant hills are hazy blue and the sweep of the first fairway is an invitation to stroll through a verdant wonderland.

On the other hand, there are times, and this was one of them, when you stand on the first tee and try to remember if you had the good sense to make a will. We stared into the jaws of hell. Lumpen grey clouds were scudding across the Thames Valley, the hills were obliterated by distant rain and the wind whistled through the bare trees and tested the efficiency of our thermal underwear. It was, whichever way you looked at it, a very ordinary day.

Straight from Laguna Quays

We'd had the odd bad day in Oz but at least the rain was warm. The best time was 500 miles north of Brisbane at a place called Laguna Quays. Here in the Australian bush and rain forest, David Graham has built a fascinating and beautiful golf course. Every hole has its own separate character and is removed from the rest of the course in the sense that it is not until you have walked off the green and through the trees that you see what is in store on the next tee.

There are bush turkeys in the undergrowth, parakeets in the forest and when the course breaks clear of the trees and skirts the coastline it runs alongside the Coral Sea, where the incoming tide engulfs the mangrove trees and makes them whisper when they eddy and sway.

In the distance there are yachts in the Whitsunday passage and distant islands shimmering in the heat haze. It is, as they say, a long way from Barnsley.

We were there to play a pro-am ahead of a skins game, i.e. prizes awarded for every hole, in which Greg Norman, Nick Price, Craig Parry and Ian Baker-Finch were playing for an absurd amount of money for a television audience daft enough to believe that the golfers would get in a flop sweat about gambling with thousands of dollars. If it is their own money at stake then you have a proper contest. If the money is provided by the sponsors then it's showbiz.

On the eve of the event we celebrated Greg Norman's birthday at a poolside party. It became rather boisterous and ended with everyone being thrown fully clothed into the swimming pool.

I mention this only to make a couple of relevant points. The first is that while I was involved in the kind of behaviour I would scold my children for, I couldn't wait to tell them that I was thrown into a swimming pool by Messrs Norman and Price. Thus does hero worship make monkeys of us all, young or old. But my real reason for reporting what happened is to record a moment of great style amid the mayhem.

Sitting at the table, aghast at what was happening around her, was the wife of one of Mr Norman's friends. She was an attractive middle-aged lady who had taken great pains to look her best. She was wearing an expensive silk suit and had obviously spent the afternoon, if not the day, at the hairdresser's. She was not the sort of person you threw into a swimming pool. Sadly, she was at the sort of party where it was difficult to make exceptions.

The more bedraggled the rest of us became the more she took on the appearance of a visiting dignitary inspecting the victims of a shipwreck. It was as uncomfortable a situation for her as it was for the rest of us. It was solved by Mr Norman who, moving behind where the lady was sitting, picked her up in her chair, carried her down the steps of the swimming pool and lowered her gently into the water.

He stopped as the water reached her shoulders, preserving for all time her dignity and those secrets that are shared only by a woman and her hairdresser. It brought forth a spontaneous burst of applause from a group of spectators who had ventured out in search of autographs.

Needless to say, those who dared to ask had their wish granted but not before taking an early bath.

The next day the gods were back on their pedestals and were booming drives down the fairways and being followed by regiments of adoring fans. Nick Price injured his wrist at practice and had to withdraw. His place was taken by David Graham, who played with borrowed clubs and won the big pot with a magnificent birdie at the seventh when he hit a four-iron from a bunker to within two feet.

'Funny game, golf,' said the television commentator. He hadn't been at the party the night before so how would he know?

My own progress round the course had been badly affected by a strange occurrence on the back nine. My opponent hit his drive into a fairway bunker and as I waited for him to play I could see he was becoming agitated.

It was a hot day so instead of walking across to see what was wrong I shouted, 'What's the problem?'

'I want to move my ball in the bunker,' he replied.

'Why?' I yelled.

'Because it's landed on a scorpion.'

I immediately gave him permission without bothering to inspect the situation in case the creature leapt from its silo and attached itself to my windpipe.

After that my game fell apart, mainly because whenever I went in a bunker I became a gibbering wreck. It wasn't until much later that I thought I might have been the victim of a cunning piece of psychological warfare.

In fact, I tested my theory on the wife by telling her the story just before we teed off at the Australian golf course in Sydney. It worked wonders. I won my first game against her in two years.

I was telling these tales as we struggled round Temple. We played ten holes before a blizzard swept in and we were blown back up the hill to the inviting bar. I am going to get the committee to build an igloo on the eighth to replace the summer house.

My plans of coming from the joys of an Australian autumn to the delights of an English spring and fine-tuning my game accordingly were in tatters. My ambition to start my English season where I had left off in Sydney by continuing my winning streak against my wife was seeming very unlikely. With weather like this, what chance do I have of convincing her that there are scorpions living in Wentworth?

April 1994

'WRINKLY' STILL DETERMINED TO CALL SHOTS ON LIFE'S BACK NINE

STANDING on the first tee at Sunningdale, Tommy Horton acknowledged the polite applause with a typical touch of his white hat and said, 'I brought the wife along to clap just in case no one turned up.' This was the first day of the Forte PGA Seniors Championship. The threeball teeing off at 9.30 a.m. had sunk a few putts in their time.

There was Horton, a rookie senior, clearly enjoying his new lease of life; Neil Coles, inscrutable of countenance, elegant of swing; and Peter Thomson, a man who won the Open five times and therefore carries with him that special aura of a sporting legend.

I had come to interview Mr Thomson who was making one of his rare appearances on an English golf course. When was he last at Sunningdale?

'Well, it's so long ago that this was a heathland course,' he said.

'What is it now?' I inquired.

'A forest,' he said. I should explain that Mr Thomson had just shot 76 and was not best pleased.

But let's go back to the beginning of the day. We assembled in the morning sun. A love of golf apart, competitors and spectators had one other common denominator – we were all aged fifty-plus. Even one or two of the caddies were using battery-operated trolleys. It was like a convention of wrinklies or a golf trip organised by Saga Holidays.

The genius of golf is that it thumbs its nose at age. It allows men like Horton, Thomson and Coles to compete with real skill and purpose, far beyond the time when participants in every other sport are past their sell-by date. Moreover it encourages those not blessed with their skill to pursue a dream of breaking 80 before they die. In any other sport the purchase of a new set of equipment after the age of fifty would be classified as a vainglorious gesture; in the case of golf it represents a sensible investment in the future.

So for those of us who believe that the back nine of life might have more to offer than we had at first been led to believe, Sunningdale was a good place to be. The Old Course at Sunningdale is my idea of perfection. Every hole poses a different problem and reveals another breathtaking vista. A mature setting suited to our mellow entourage.

It was the first course Peter Thomson played when he

arrived in England from Australia in 1951. It has remained a favourite ever since. Thomson was one of the players who provided the foundation of the modern multi-million dollar industry called golf. He won a hat-trick of Opens in '54, '55 and '56. The following year he finished runner-up to Bobby Locke. In 1958 he won it again.

The critics said these victories didn't count for much because the great Americans were not competing at the time. In 1965 he answered them by winning at Royal Birkdale in a field containing all the top Americans including Tony Lema, the holder, Arnold Palmer and Jack Nicklaus. When he joined the American Seniors Tour as he turned fifty, he won eleven tournaments in thirteen months. He was a pioneer of the Asian tour, a pithy commentator, a journalist and erstwhile politician. He is one of those nuggety Australians who only speak when they have something useful to say and who observe the world through shrewd eyes. Nowadays he builds golf courses, with twenty projects on the go including the new Duke's course at St Andrews – 'A great honour,' he says.

He was and is a maverick, a man set apart by his ruthless ambition to succeed. It made him successful but it didn't win him many charm contests. Gary Player wrote of him: '...he was aloof and could be very sarcastic at times. It always seemed to me that he wanted to reveal his superiority and knowledge to people.'

One incident particularly narked Player. The South African took twenty-nine hours of air travel to get from

France to Melbourne but in spite of the delays got off the plane, went on the course and won what he thought was the most amazing triumph of his career. Thomson remarked, 'What's so amazing about that? You were sitting down and resting all the time in the plane, weren't you?'

Judged by our talk I wouldn't say that Peter Thomson has allowed old age to soften him. Physically he is much the same. Broad shoulders, narrow hips, slight fold at the belly but not too much to worry about. He has started writing his life story. He didn't bother during the years when he was a superstar golfer, the time when he might have cashed in on it. Why didn't he write it then?

'I've not grown up until recently,' he said.

Similarly when, after winning his third Open title he was asked to write a golf instruction book he declined. Why?

'Because I didn't think I knew enough. Still don't.'

Starting his autobiography has meant asking questions about himself and what happened. Cricket was his first love. He wanted to be a leg-spin bowler, like Shane Warne. His mother went to an aunt who read the tea leaves. She saw the young Thomson standing triumphant in a green field. She said he would be famous throughout the world. Mrs Thomson took this to mean that her son would captain the Australian cricket team. She didn't tell him in case it turned his head. She finally told him about his aunt's prediction when he was fifty.

He came to golf by chance.

'I had bandy legs. My mother was told by doctors to

put my legs in irons. She thought this was pretty radical. She took me to a physiotherapist. In those days they were treated like witch doctors. He told her that what I needed was long walks. I used to go with my uncle and his dogs and walk the golf course. It started from that. I didn't have any heroes. The men were at war, there was no one to learn from. I just picked the game up myself. I've never had a lesson, no one taught me how. I have a suspicion about the coaching that goes on nowadays. I think it ruins young players. You have to be self-reliant to play golf well. That's the key to it, you have to do things for yourself.

'I went to America when I was twenty-one and saw Sam Snead and Ben Hogan play. I learned more by watching them and players like Bobby Locke than any coach could possibly have taught me. I wanted to be like Hogan. He played like a machine. He would go a whole round without hitting one bad shot. The rest were slapdash by comparison. I set my sights up there.

'When I came to England the difference between myself and people like Dai Rees and others was that they were club pros and relied on what they made at the clubs for a living. I had nothing. I had to win tournaments to pay the rent. It instils in you a powerful need to win'.

For winning an average tournament he was paid £300. Winning the Open earned him £750. When he totted up at the end of a successful season he would have made about £3,000. Nonetheless, he doesn't moan about the money in modern golf.

'Let the golfers have it. Otherwise who takes it? The agents, those people on the edge of the game. They're not important. I don't think I was born too soon. I won enough to live comfortably. I've made enough to spend what I want and know there's more where that came from. Money isn't everything. When someone says that you can be sure they have plenty,' he said with a rare smile.

The changes in the game?

'Golf courses. Some designers have a terrible ego problem. They design courses for Open championships, courses that would be tough for the likes of Faldo and Norman. They think of themselves as being wimpish if someone goes round their course in 64 or so. The great art of designing is to make the course suitable to all kinds of golfer.

'Coaching has become big business. I count myself lucky that I received no coaching. Children should be left to their own devices. In Australia we have the Institute for Sport. There are six hundred coaches, it costs thirty-six million Australian dollars a year. That money should go into grassroots sport providing facilities at schools. I'm against spending money to create a sporting élite.

'I think the biggest difference in golf in my time has been the change in the golf ball. The larger ball has made it much easier to play and taken some of the subtlety out of the game. It's bigger and heavier and it doesn't move in the wind like the small ball used to. My suggestion would be to make the ball a couple of pennyweights lighter and then we'll see a difference,' he said.

Gary Player called Peter Thomson 'the best I have ever seen with the small ball on a links course'. His record gives him an unchallenged place in the Pantheon.

He remains unconvinced about something as fanciful as his own legendary status. He was keen to get back to his book, finding the voyage of discovery 'very therapeutic'. What would he call it? 'Oh, I haven't really thought about that,' he said. 'Nothing fancy,' he added. What a good title.

August 1993

CLIENTS CLAMOUR FOR THE ANGULAR THEORIES OF THE KING OF SWING

D AVID LEADBETTER has a demanding kind of fame. When people recognise him, they request something more than an autograph. They ask him to spend a moment or two watching their golf swing so they might become better players.

'It happens all the time,' he says. 'Airports are particular traps. I'm running for a plane and someone says, "Hey, Dave, good to see ya. Spare a minute to check over my swing?" And, right there and then, they take an imaginary club and hit a drive down the departure hall.'

This happens to David Leadbetter wherever he goes in the world. He is the most famous golf coach on the planet, the only one as famous as his clients. He may not earn their money but who does? In any event, he isn't grumbling. His videos are bestsellers, so are his books. He has David Leadbetter golf academies in America, Malaysia and Europe and he has just opened a new one at Chart Hills, in Biddendam, Kent. He employs thirty teachers throughout the world. He works with twenty professional golfers on the American circuit and twelve in Europe.

His promotional material refers to him as 'The King of Swing', which is a bit of a cheek if you happen to be a fan of Benny Goodman. Anyone old enough to understand the last observation will also know what I mean when I say that David Leadbetter looks like Cardew 'The Cad' Robinson. He is a tall, angular man; everything about him is lean and knobbly. When he talks, he is forever exercising his fingers. They look as if they might be double-jointed.

He says 'Hey' a lot, as in 'I thought about playing in Europe but, hey, America is where the action is,' or 'Something inside of me said, hey, that's the wrong choice.' He is friendly and approachable, which is why people stop him in the street and ask him to make them better golfers.

'People think you're a miracle worker. Touch them, lay on the hands and behold, they have a golf swing. You give them a quick fix, they go out on the course and hit one good shot and think they've cracked it. The fact is, the average amateur doesn't realise how hard the pro works,' he says.

In his book *The Golf Swing*, which, if you were so inclined, you could read in eight languages, Leadbetter explains why the seemingly simple proposition of hitting a stationary ball is so complicated.

'With a hitting surface on the clubface of 2.5 inches, you have to strike a ball only 1.68 inches in diameter. The

14.25 ounce club, which builds up a dynamic pulling weight of approximately 100lbs during your 1.5 second motion, has to be swung at a speed of approaching 90mph through an arc of approximately 18 feet.

'The ball is on the surface for just 0.00035 of a second and, to be hit the desired distance in the right direction, has to be launched at an angle of 42 degrees.'

This does not take into account wind, rain or the fact your ball is lying in a divot and you are suffering from a hangover.

The men whose job it is to unravel the mysteries of hitting a golf ball in the direction you desire are the gurus of sport. There is no other game where so many rely on so few, where – in extreme cases – the golf teacher takes on the mystical qualities of a witch doctor or a faith healer.

There is no other game where an industry as sophisticated as that which put men on the moon has been created to put pimples on golf balls, grooves on club heads, broom handles on putters and much else besides

to allow the amateur golfer his vain pursuit of perfection. But technology is not enough.

'It's amazing that given the improved equipment people play with and the better conditions of golf courses, the general standard of play remains what it was, say, twenty-five years ago,' said Leadbetter. Why?

'The reason there are a lot of duffers out there is that most people don't understand the golf swing. Most people swing as if they are digging for worms. They don't bother to learn the rudiments of the game. Most people think if they play once a week and have a lesson now and again that will make them into a good player. It won't,' he said.

In Florida, where he lives, he advertised in his local paper for golfers to take part in an experiment. They ranged from single-figure players to one or two with 36 handicaps. He put them through routines of fitness training, coaching and sessions with a sports psychologist. All improved but the high handicappers the most dramatically. One man whose best score had been 105 was breaking 90 on a regular basis. I asked David Leadbetter what this proved.

'That everyone can get better with the proper coaching,' he said.

But perhaps not everyone has the ambition to improve? Perhaps most of us enjoy being duffers? Mr Leadbetter gave me an old-fashioned look.

'I think that nowadays golf is much more than a game. It's a lifestyle. It means so much to people, so why not play it as well as you can? If you learn the rudiments of the game, you're going to enjoy it more and if you enjoy your golf, perhaps you might enjoy everything more. A happy golfer is a happy person,' he said.

Leadbetter grew up in Rhodesia with Mark McNulty and Nick Price. He played the pro circuit for a while but Price recalls, that he was always to be found with his nose in a golf instruction book, learning about the game. When Leadbetter turned to full-time teaching, Price was his first star client. Faldo followed and his reputation was consolidated.

Price says Leadbetter's greatest gift as a teacher is in spotting quickly what is wrong and then making the player understand why he has a problem.

I watched him working with Peter Baker. He picked up the fault immediately and gave him one thought to work on. Instantly, the player began to hit the ball differently.

'When I first started teaching, I gave too much information. It was like giving a prescription and telling them to take all the pills at once. Nowadays when I coach I feed the knowledge intravenously, a little at a time,' he said.

He is imaginative in his use of teaching aids. According to Faldo, when Leadbetter was remodelling his swing, they used rubber bands, medicine balls, water wings, towels and fishing rods to achieve what Leadbetter calls 'feeling'.

'If anyone saw what we got up to, they would say we were off our rockers,' said Faldo.

David Leadbetter's critics – and they are plentiful, as you might imagine with someone as successful as he –

claim that not only are his methods crazy, but they have created a generation of golfers who are thoroughly confused by an over-application of perplexing technique.

I once composed a humorous article about Leadbetter's teaching methods and four or five teaching professionals wrote serious letters to me making the point that his teaching was more confusing than funny. One said he was delighted that Leadbetter's disciples taught the way they did because it meant more work for him sorting out deranged golfers.

'I have never said there's only one way to teach. All I know about teaching is that individual people have their own particular needs. Critics don't bother me. I didn't set out to be high profile but, because of my association with the two Nicks, I started getting publicity. I think it has enabled people to see golf teachers in a better light. It has been good for teachers as a whole. I think people say, hey, if Nick Price and Nick Faldo can work at the game, then so can I,' he said.

I asked him if he had ever looked at a golfer and given up. If he said 'No' I was thinking of showing him my swing. He said that some golfers could suffer such a lack of confidence that they were beyond teaching – not for ever, but the process could not start until they sorted themselves out.

I asked him who were the best people to work with, apart from the pros. He said that Geoffrey Boycott was a model pupil. Now this was interesting. Only a few days before I interviewed Leadbetter, I had watched Boycott win a two-day tournament on the West Course at Wentworth. Playing off a handicap of 11, he dropped eight shots in two rounds of golf. His caddie said he had seen pros play worse.

Kenny Lynch, one of his playing partners on the last day, while admiring Boycott's play, was not happy with his meticulous and painstaking progress around the golf course. When interviewed at the end of his round, Mr Lynch said that he imagined it would have been more fun playing with the National Front.

However, David Leadbetter has nothing but praise for his pupil.

'Boycott's mental attitude is exemplary. He understands the fundamentals of the swing, he loves practising. He's a joy to teach. Had he taken up golf instead of cricket, there is little doubt he would have made a very fine professional player,' he said.

I thanked him for the information because I have a game of golf against Boycott coming up and, if he thinks he is playing off 11 after what I have heard then he can find another sucker.

When I first arrived to interview David Leadbetter, I came across Ken Schofield, chief executive of the European Tour. He asked me what I was doing and I said I was looking for David Leadbetter. Ken said, 'I hope you find him because if you don't, about forty of our players will have nervous breakdowns.'

David Leadbetter is an important figure in the history of golf because he symbolises the mystery that is at the heart of the game as well as representing the means by which we attempt to find a solution. His critics would argue that what he typifies is the period in the game when man learned how to play like a robot and flair and enjoyment were taken from golf.

Whatever the truth, David Leadbetter has the prospect of future fame and riches without a foreseeable horizon. I mean, if you can go on earning millions playing golf as long as Arnold Palmer, how much longer might you last teaching it? Hey.

September 1994

In 1998 Leadbetter and his star pupil Nick Faldo parted company in controversial fashion. Leadbetter was upset by the impersonal way he was sacked by a golfer he had not only helped to success but who had become a friend. Nonetheless, putting rejection and disappointment aside, Leadbetter remains the number one golfing guru.

LET'S DO WHAT COMES NATURALLY – HIT THE BALL

H AS IT ever struck you as downright peculiar that in spite of a multi-billion dollar industry being involved in making golfers better players the vast majority have handicaps of 22 and above? In other words, never in the history of sporting endeavour has so much been dedicated to so many with such little effect.

It is my belief that it is the golfer in possession of the largest amount of new technology who has the most problems. The overloaded bag is also a certain indication that, under the owner's cap, his brain is similarly stuffed with confusing theory.

Nowadays, the advice comes at the golfer from every angle and source but, while there might be a lot of it, not much of it is working. Otherwise the Japanese would be better players than they are, we would be able to play a fourball in less time than it takes to fly to Moscow and David Leadbetter would be out of a job.

Mention of the aforesaid Mr Leadbetter set me thinking. I read that one of our foremost teachers of the old school, Ken Adwick, thought that much of modern golf teaching is confusing, and unnecessarily so. Mr Adwick, who taught the likes of Jacklin, Nicklaus and Player, said, 'This isn't sour grapes but I wish I could keep count of how many weekend players I've had to sort out after they studied pictures and tapes of Leadbetter and other gurus.'

The fact is most golfers want to play the game once or twice a week and regularly break 90 when they do. They want to arrive at that state of bliss without having a brainstorm or putting their back out. My suspicion of the disciples of the new progressive theories of golf, and what they get up to, started a few years ago when I went to collect my wife from a coaching lesson.

Imagine my chagrin when I came across her with arms pinioned to her sides trying to swing a golf club. More disturbing, was the fact that she was gripping a medicine ball between her knees. Now where I come from, this would have warranted a visit from the vice squad. When I asked what was going on, I was told this was an exercise to enable the golfer to maintain the proposed posture at address. I drove the pupil home and contemplated the kind of counselling given when a member of the family joins the Moonies.

Playing a game with friends the other day, I noticed my partner had a card clipped to his bag on which he had listed the main points he had to remember before he swung the club. There were twenty headings. The pilot of a jumbo jet has less to worry about before he safely delivers 400 passengers and several tons of metal on to the tarmac.

This set me thinking of the kind of information I had absorbed about the game from various sources over the years, and what I had been programmed to remember every time I picked up a golf club.

First of all, the grip. I was told not to grip the club too fiercely, to imagine it was a dove in my hands and I was throttling it but not taking its head off. Then the hands should not be too far from the body. Imagine if you are a man, you are having a pee and that is where the hands should be. All important is body posture over the ball. Ideally, I was to imagine that I was perched on a bar stool while leaning over a fence.

Remember the take-away must be smooth and flowing. Imagine you have a bucket of water in your hands. If you can take it back from the address without spilling any, that is what is required.

Alternatively, you can imagine yourself to be a windmill, or a particularly interesting image is to picture yourself with your head through a pane of glass and able to swing the club without breaking anything.

I've never been able to understand that one, but the advice remains stuck to my brain like grease on a plate. At the top of the backswing with the club head pointing at the target, don't forget that the back leg should be rigid as if encased in plaster. Or that's what I was told.

I was also advised that to facilitate the proper action in the down swing I must transfer the weight from the leg in the plaster cast to the leg without one. It would help, or so they said, if I imagined pulling a rope with a bell on it.

So what we have so far is a man sitting on a bar stool

leaning over a fence while taking a leak, with his head stuck through a pane of glass and one leg in plaster. That's only the half of it and I still haven't hit the ball.

My proposition is that any human activity broken down into separate movements and analysed in such detail would become much more difficult than it ought to be, not to mention less pleasurable.

If, for instance, David Leadbetter and his disciples turned to another area of human activity that is over-loaded with advice, that of sexual relations, think of the consequences. Imagine the confusion as the couples struggled to understand the principles of torque, the techniques of weight transference, not to mention the advisability of clearing the leading hip at the moment of impact.

Enough is enough. It is time someone spoke up for doing what comes naturally. When John Major sounded the clarion call for getting Back to Basics, I think, as a sporting man, he had golf in mind.

So the next time you stand on the tee, I want you to free your brain of all the technical clutter, the mystical mumbo-jumbo. All you have to remember is the advice of the Scottish professional who said, 'The right way to play golf is to go up and hit the bloody thing.'

Whatever happens after that will be covered by the old maxim: 'Win some, lose some'. Thus might we be saved from the ludicrous proposition of seeking perfection, which makes millionaires of gurus and suckers of the rest of us.

September 1994

MASTER COMMUNICATOR
WHO HAS ENJOYED
A LONG LIFE ENHANCED
BY FUN AND GAMES

ALISTAIR COOKE was twelve years old when he met Neville Cardus. He saw the great man walking around the ground at the Blackpool cricket festival. Cooke read Cardus every morning in the *Manchester Guardian* but never imagined they would meet. He approached him and asked for his autograph.

'I had a little green autograph book. Cardus wore a floppy hat with the brim turned down like Crocodile Dundee, pipe, tweed jacket, flannels. He signed my book and if I close my eyes I can transcribe his signature,' he said.

It was 1920, the year after prohibition was introduced in America and the writer and critic H. L. Mencken described the legislation as 'Puritanism, the haunting fear that someone, somewhere, might be happy.' Although he wasn't to know it at the time, both America and Mencken were going to play a far more significant part in Cooke's life than Blackpool or Neville Cardus.

Thirty years later, after Cooke had reported in the *Manchester Guardian* on the epic fight in New York between Sugar Ray Robinson and Randolph Turpin, Cardus wrote a fan letter to Cooke. In it he said that he carried Cooke's article with him at all times and brought it out whenever people wanted to know how a boxing match should be reported. Flattered by the letters Cooke replied saying that he had once, as a small boy, obtained Cardus's autograph. Came the reply: 'Dear Mr Cooke, many thanks for your letter. I am glad you have my autograph because now I have yours.'

Today, aged eighty-six, Alistair Cooke allows himself a smile at the memory. He is spending some time in London meeting friends and publicising a book called *Fun and Games with Alistair Cooke*. It is a collection of his sports writing and includes the report that so

impressed Cardus. People might be surprised at Cooke's range of sporting interests. In the book he writes about cricket, soccer, boxing, baseball, horse racing and, best and most lovingly of all, about golf.

He says in his introduction: 'For more than fifty years I can truly say that scarcely has a day gone by when I didn't think about government, its plethora of ailments and its depressing range of failed panaceas. In games the problems are solved, somebody wins. Hence the "isle of joy" offered by sport in an ocean of anxieties. I have come to feel a deep, unspoken pity for people who have no attachment to a single sport, almost as sorry for them as I am for teetotallers.'

I have known him a good few years now and when people ask 'What is he like?' I can only answer that what you hear is what you get. In conversation he shapes stories and observations exactly as he does on radio in *Letter From America*. He starts with a simple thought, wanders around the world and then returns to base. It is like watching a wonderful piece of pottery being shaped before your eyes. He looks an inquisitive man, long sharp nose, watchful pale eyes. The body is bent but still stoking enough energy to play a regular round of golf and, of course, work.

Next year Alistair Cooke will celebrate embarking upon his fiftieth year of *Letter From America*. The series is the longest running one-man programme in the history of broadcasting and it is heard in fifty-two countries. It is a weekly demonstration of the craft of a born journalist blessed with a unique style. Kenneth Tynan said: 'Cooke is one of the great reporters. Nobody can reproduce the events, giving it feel as well as the facts, the pith as well as the husk, with greater clarity or gentler wit.' Paraphrasing Tynan's observation about a great actor I once wrote: 'If there is a tightrope bridging the gap between a good journalist and a great one, Alistair Cooke would make the trip in white tie and tails with a cocktail in one hand and a quill in the other.'

When we met he was wearing an old cardigan with a hole in the left elbow. He made it look as much a fashion accessory as torn jeans. I told him that I remembered the report of the Robinson – Turpin fight and it stayed in my mind as it had with Cardus. He said, 'It was 1951 and I was in California covering the Japanese peace talks. At the time there was another marvellous story in the area called the central valley project where they were reversing the flow of two rivers to provide power in California. At the same time Sugar Ray was fighting Turpin in New York. I cabled A.P. Wadsworth, the editor of the *Manchester Guardian*, a marvellous man with a great sense of humour. I told him I intended to stay in California to report "the greatest hydro-electric project there has been" rather than cover a prizefight. He cabled back: ' "Go to New York immediately. In this country blood is thicker than water." '

Wadsworth was right because Cooke's report of the fight would justify its place in any anthology of sports writing you care to mention. It is not only great reporting, it is memorable prose: 'Turpin seemed almost sick with the concentration of his own frenzy. But he stayed with it and flung all he knew. His left eye was showering blood so that the four gloves looked as if they had been dipped in paint. Turpin's gloves were up against the hailstones rattling round his head. Then they were down, and limp and gone forever. Two, three, four more rocketing blows and Turpin was slipping against the rope, baying mutely at the nearly full moon and the roaring thousands up against it. And then the man in white came in. And it was all over.'

I asked Cooke if Cardus had been an influence in his career.

'Well, I read him as a young person so I suppose so but I wasn't persuaded to copy his style. Very high style wasn't it? Typical of the *Guardian* at the time. Very literary. Don't think it would work nowadays. James Agate was a great devotee of Cardus. I once sat with C.B. Fry, Plum Warner and Agate at Lord's and we started picking the All Time England cricket team. We all put Frank Woolley, the great Kent stylist, in the team. Then Agate came out with this theory that Woolley never existed, that he was an invention of the wretched Cardus. Cardus created him out of descriptions like "in the butterfly melancholy of the evening Woolley came to the crease. His strokes had all the beauty of Debussy." Well I saw him bat three times and I didn't hear any Debussy.'

The man who had as much as anyone to do with the shaping of Cooke's style was one of his tutors at Cambridge, Arthur Quiller-Couch, who wrote under the name 'Q'. Cooke remembers: 'One day I went to collect an essay I had sent to him, convinced that it was the most brilliant article that he, Q, or anyone else, had ever written on the subject. He was dressing for dinner and he dressed down, which is to say he started at the neck and clothed himself downwards. Therefore he was fully dressed except for shoes and trousers as he flicked through my essay. He came to the third page which I knew was the greatest piece of writing ever committed to one page of paper. He studied it and shook his head.

"My dear Cooke", he said. "You must learn how to murder your darlings." I have never forgotten that advice, the best any writer, particularly a journalist, can ever receive.'

But back to Cardus. There is little doubt that he and Cooke were the greatest names the *Guardian* possessed. Cardus was the first to be knighted. Cooke, because he is an American citizens was granted an honorary KBE. It means he can put the initials after his name but not 'Sir' before it.

His best story about Cardus concerns Emmott Robinson, the aggressive Yorkshire bowler of the twenties whom Cardus admired for his resolute spirit and feisty temperament. Nonetheless it didn't stop Cardus criticising the bowler nor offering him advice on technical matters. After one such article in which Cardus made several observations on how Robinson might amend his technique, the bowler was sitting watching play when a friend sat next to him and asked: 'Did you see what Cardus wrote about you this morning?' And Emmott said, 'I did that.' His friend asked, 'And what did you think about it?' and Emmott paused and thought for a long time and then said, 'I'd like to bowl at t'bugger.'

Alistair Cooke took up golf in his fifties. It was his wife who persuaded him, saying that if he didn't he would end up 'a typewriter arthritic'. His teacher on Long Island was an old Scottish pro called George Heron.

When he first went to meet Mr Heron, he watched a while as the pro gave a putting lesson to a small, thick-set man in a white cap.

'I was fascinated,' said Cooke. 'I didn't realise you needed a lesson to putt. At the end Heron said, 'I hope that has been a help Ben.' Of course the pupil was the great Ben Hogan. Some time later I read Ben Hogan's statement that if you were to pick up a golf club and swing it in a natural manner you would become the worst golfer in the world. He said you had to learn to master twelve unnatural muscular movements. I was much taken by that. Then I saw Hogan after he had won the US Open by six strokes standing on the practice tee hitting shot after shot at the pin. Everyone had gone home but here was the man who had won still practising. When asked why, he said "I hit a bad seven-iron on the twelfth hole and I'm just putting things right." So with all that in mind, I learned to play the game correctly and well.

'When I was fifty-eight years old I reached 11 handicap. George Heron said there wasn't an earthly reason why I should ever play above 12. But it didn't happen. I remember the period when not breaking 90 was a disaster. Nowadays, if I couldn't putt it I'd never break 100.'

Cooke says that his great friend and 'guru', H.L. Mencken, wrote the pithiest epigram about golf.

'He said, "If I had my way anyone guilty of golf would be denied all offices of trust under these United States." When he was dying, I sat down and wrote through the night an appreciation for the *Manchester Guardian*.

'It was five thousand words long. It was 1948 and in those days papers were rationed. Four pages for half the week but on Tuesday, Thursday and Saturday increased to six pages. I cabled Wadsworth, my editor, warning him my appreciation to be published upon the announcement of my friend's death was a long one. He cabled back: "Hope he dies Monday, Wednesday or Friday." '

Cooke ponders the decline of public manners.

'Here's an old man's statement: "The young today are casual, bad mannered and have no respect for the old." Well I didn't make that up. Socrates did. So it's been a problem for a long time now,' he said.

Nonetheless he wonders about the effect that fame and fortune (mainly fortune) can have on even intelligent tennis stars like Boris Becker, whom he started off admiring and now regards as 'nuisance'. He recalls that he was once talking to Jack Nicklaus about John McEnroe's appalling conduct on court. Nicklaus said, 'The guy to blame is the father. When I was about eleven years old I threw a club. My father said, "Jack, if you do that again you won't play golf for six months." I sulked and went to my room. He came after me, opened the door and said, "What would Mr Jones think?" Bobby Jones was my dad's idol. I never threw another club.'

What Nicklaus said gave Alistair Cooke an idea. He remembered a sentence and wrote to Mr McEnroe Snr.

'I said, "Here is a sentence once written by the immortal Bobby Jones. I thought you might like to have it done in needlepoint and mounted in a suitable frame to hang over Little John's bed." It says: "The rewards of golf – and of life too, I expect – are worth very little if you don't play the game by the etiquette as well as the rules." I never heard back from Mr McEnroe Snr. I can only assume the letter went astray.'

I don't think you can interview Alistair Cooke; rather you let him muse about the nature of things for a while. He has one such final musing before I leave. It concerns his friend and golfing partner Manheim.

They planned a golfing holiday and were given an introduction through a friend to a very select club. Alistair called to make the booking.

'Pleasure to have you with us Mr Cooke,' the secretary said. 'What is the name of your partner?' Alistair told him his friend was called Manheim. A short time later the secretary called him back. 'We have been looking through our register of players and we don't appear to have any of the sort of gentleman you describe as members of the club,' he said.

'I didn't describe my friend as a matter of fact. But he is Jewish so if you don't want Jews at your club then we shall go and play elsewhere,' said Cooke.

Some time later Manheim was told by a friend that he could arrange for him to play at the exclusive Jewish Club in Palm Beach. Manheim called.

'Certainly Mr Manheim,' they said. 'And your friend's name?'

'Cooke,' said Manheim. 'Alistair Cooke.' There was a sharp intake of breath at the other end of the line.

'Oh dear, that could be trouble,' they said.

Cooke shrugs and smiles at the sheer bloody stupidity of it all. But that's the way it is and, no doubt, the way it will always be. Like all the best commentators he is critical but rarely censorious, a fastidious man but not po-faced. He keeps a wise and amused eye on the world.

'Any ambitions left?' I ask. Ordinarily it would be daft to ask this question of an eighty-six year old but not Alistair Cooke.

'I hope in fourteen years time to play to my age round a golf course,' he said.

November 1994

Reformed Barnes
in Second Chance
Saloon

WHEN Brian Barnes, professional golfer, was Good Old Barnesy, professional pisspot, this is what he used to do.

'Let's say my tee-off time was 8.30 in the morning. When I awoke I'd stick the kettle on and have three or four large brandies with my morning coffee. That would get me on to the putting green. Then I would fill a litre bottle with a mixture of two-thirds vodka and one-third orange juice. That would get me round the golf course,' he said. I asked him what he did when he had finished playing. 'That's when the serious drinking started,' he said.

At fifty he went to America seeking a new career on the Seniors' Tour. It was in every sense a second chance for Brian Barnes because he gave up drink and there is time yet to make up for those wasted years both as a man and as a golfer. Drink brought him to the edge. Literally. Twice he drove to Beachy Head in the grip of a severe depression and contemplated committing suicide. He revved the car while he made the decision. 'Thank God I lacked the guts to do it,' he says.

The crucial incident that made him seek medical advice instead of oblivion through drink was when he drove his car at breakneck speeds though narrow country lanes near his home angered by his wife's observation that he was too drunk to drive.

'I arrived at the pub, took one sip of a drink and was violently ill at the thought of what I had done,' he said. 'I went for treatment in a clinic. I had five weeks' group therapy. They told me that had I carried on I would have killed myself in three months. When I came out of the closet and confessed I was an alcoholic, colleagues who had played with me for years on the tour said, "We never saw you pissed,"' he said. They were probably sparing his blushes. His reputation was that of a boozing, boisterous fellow whose sometimes bizarre behaviour on the

golf course had more to do with an excess of drink than a genuinely eccentric nature.

When he shot 62 at Dalmahoy in the 1981 Players' Championship, the last of his seventeen victories throughout the world in thirty years as a professional golfer, he enjoyed 'a little carry out' of six pints. He then downed another eight before winning the play-off. At the same course in the same year, when winning the Scottish Professional Championship, he marked his ball on the eighteenth green with a beer can. The officials shook their heads. The galleries laughed and called him 'Good Old Barnsey'.

He says, 'It was always "Good Old Barnesy. He's a lad isn't he?" In fact, I was in deep trouble. I wasn't a fighting drunk. Booze made me easygoing, the life and soul of the party. I am a shy person, lacking in confidence. I drank to feel better. Fact is I never had a hangover. When I was thirteen I weighed 13 stone and stood 6ft 2in tall. I could drink six pints of scrumpy and not fall down.

'Golf was a very social game. I remember when I was a young pro going to a seminar about golfers and health. The doctor who was advising us said he thought that four to five pints a day wouldn't do us any harm, nor twenty to thirty cigs. Times change.'

He didn't have a festering ambition to play golf. He played his first games as a child in Germany where his father, who had the job of repatriating foreigners at the end of the war, built a golf course. Brian Barnes was a strong, athletic boy who loved cricket and rugby. He went on a sports scholarship to Millfield where R.J.O.

Meyer, the prescient headmaster, insisted he take up golf seriously. 'You will play golf whether you like to or not,' said Jack Meyer. At seventeen, Barnes was down to a three handicap, two years later he was plus one.

When he joined the European Tour he danced many a merry jig. He was a swashbuckler on the course, smiting the ball miles off the tee, never taking a backward step when the time came to attack. It was a laugh a minute, the enjoyment shared by golfer and spectator alike. And the boy could play at the highest level and in the best of company.

In 1970 he played the American Tour. In 1975 he became the only man who can claim to have beaten Jack Nicklaus twice in one day in the Ryder Cup. Nicklaus remains a friend and a hero. Barnes signed with the great man's management company for his venture in the States.

'Jack once gave me the most terrible bollocking for not choosing a career in the States. He said my game was made for American courses. He said it was a terrible waste.' I asked him if he felt that he had chucked away his career. 'I don't think so. In fact I can't afford to look back. Who knows what might happen in the next ten years.

'Sometimes I do wonder what might have been had I not been pissed most of the time. Gary Player once gave me a dressing down. Asked me if I ever thought what I could have achieved had I been different. I asked him if he'd ever considered what sort of golfer he might have been had he been 6ft 2in tall. He laughed.

'What I don't know is if I had enough guts in me to win

a major. It takes guts you know. I used to like coming
from the back to win but I wonder if I could have done it
from the front, leading all the way and winning. I have
always suffered from never believing I had the ability.
Most champions don't have self-doubt. Most champions
are plain bloody selfish, don't give a toss. My problem
has always been that I never liked to disappoint people.'

When I met Barnes he was practising his putting at
West Chiltington Club in Sussex, which he designed and
helped build. He is a tall man with a solid build and a face
that smiles easily, the sort of man you would like to have
a drink with at the local pub. We drove to his home
nearby, through lanes thick with blossom and budding
rhododendron, to a front door framed by wisteria.

His wife, Hillary, is slender, attractive and charming. It
is difficult to imagine that anyone could become befuddled enough to want to leave all this and drive off
Beachy Head. But then booze does terrible things to
people.

Brian Barnes said, 'When it was at its worst, there was
no light at the end of the tunnel. I didn't want to get out
of bed.' He paused, seeking the words to describe what it
used to be like. Finally he said, 'It was a vicious thing.'

Nowadays, supported by family and friends, he treads
the fragile tightrope that is never-ending for alcoholics.

'The best part is I now have the best possible get-out
for leaving boring cocktail parties early,' he said. 'I have
never liked cocktail chit-chat. When I was drinking I'd
just get pissed. Now I've got a doctor's note so I leave
early. So far, stopping drinking has not been a problem ...

yet. That's a big word in an alcoholic's vocabulary ...yet.'

It is not going to be easy for Brian Barnes as he seeks a new life and, I suspect, redemption in America.

'People imagine it's going to be a pushover. In fact it is going to be really tough,' he said.

Golf apart, there are new pressures and temptations to combat. Barnes has taken a friend along who is as much a minder and a caddie. There will be a lot of people rooting for this agreeable and talented man, hoping that he succeeds and prospers.

'I hope it works out. I have worked harder recently than ever before. I am swinging better than at any time in my career. You could say I have mellowed,' he said. Better than ending up pickled, which is where he was heading.

June 1995

Brian Barnes made a success in America. In June 1998, his fourth season on the US Seniors' Tour, he won the Canada Open in Calgary. He followed this by finishing fourth in the US Seniors' Open and in the final event of the season, the Pacific Bell Seniors' Classic, tied for third spot. That season he won more than half a million dollars. Altogether he has earned nearly $2 million in his new career. In 1999 he was frustrated by illness and injuries.

DAVIES DRIVES A WEDGE INTO GOLF'S CHAUVINISM

MARK MCCORMACK had this great idea. Why not invite Laura Davies to play a golf tournament against three men off the back tees and see what happens. It would intrigue the world of golf and might prove a significant skirmish in the battle of the sexes. There are, after all, large numbers of men throughout the world who believe women should be allowed on a golf course only at certain times, preferably between dusk and dawn.

In Australia, women golfers are called 'associates', presumably because the committee doesn't know what a woman looks like.

So when Laura Davies stood on the first tee at The Pines golf course at Sanctuary Cove in Queensland in the company of John Daly, Tom Watson and Peter Senior, there was much more at stake than a jackpot of £75,000. Beforehand she rejected any suggestion that her presence in the tournament had more significance than a game of golf. She didn't want to be used as a figurehead in the debate about golfing equality. But she couldn't deny that her presence attracted many more women than normally attend these events and while their support was not entirely political, there was a palpable desire for Laura to succeed on behalf of all women golfers.

She said she was so nervous waiting to tee off she nearly fainted. She could hardly take her club back and slap the drive down the fairway. She hit her second into the bunker, played an exquisite sand shot and made the putt for a par. It was enough to win her the hole and £2,500, this being a skins game, whereby there is prize money on every hole.

It was the best possible start. When she called her mother that night to report on the day's events, she told her she thought that perhaps her opponents had let her win the hole to settle her down.

If that had been true – and it wasn't – they would soon have been regretting their generosity as Davies played wonderful, attacking golf, never yielding a yard to the men off the tee and sometimes out-driving them, even John Daly.

Her talent transformed what could have been a disastrous sporting gimmick into a fascinating contest. A lot of golfers, particularly in the upper reaches of the professional game, where psychobabble is rife, would do well to sack their gurus and watch Davies instead.

Hers is a simple and uncomplicated approach to golf. She plays as if she enjoys it which, when all is said and done, is the main purpose of any game. This proposition will come as a surprise to many golfers, who would like us to believe that they are involved in a profession as arduous and stressful as it is significant.

Davies would have nothing to do with this pretentious baloney. She believes golf is fun and better than working in a supermarket. Since she has done both, she is in a better position to make a judgment than many of her kind, who venture into the outside world only when their ball goes out of bounds.

She didn't start playing golf until she was fourteen. She was scratch at seventeen and plus five when she turned pro. She has never had a lesson in her life. Her entire game is based on watching great golfers and learning from them. She confessed to Tom Watson that he was one of the people she copies. Having met Watson and played with him, her next ambition is a dream fourball with Seve Ballesteros, Fred Couples and Jack Nicklaus. Then, she says, she could die happy.

Watching Davies, Watson, Senior and Daly was to understand the unique capacity golf has to accommodate people of differing shape, size and sex. Here was a woman playing on equal terms with men and a forty-six year old against a man seventeen years his junior. In many ways, the contrast between Tom Watson and John Daly was the most absorbing aspect of the match.

Watson's golf is chamber music. His supporters quote Longhurst and wear designer golf gear. Daly's golf is rock 'n' roll, his supporters a personal barmy army. Watson won five British Opens and is in the late autumn of a majestic career. He has his own place in Golf's Hall of Fame. Daly has won one Open. He could win more, depending on which is the greater – his talent for golf or his capacity for self-destruction.

It will be a pity if he allows his demons to overwhelm his great gifts. It is for certain golf has seen nothing like him. Jack Newton, who knows a golfer when he sees one, watched Daly at work yesterday and said he had never seen hitting like it.

The Pines is a long and tough course. Daly trashed it. On the ninth, a par five measuring more than 600 yards, he took a driver and a one-iron to reach the green. The fifteenth hole, a 450 yard par four, he conquered with a drive and a sand wedge. At the seventeenth, another par five approaching 600 yards in length, he hit a one-iron from an awkward lie over a stretch of water as wide as the English Channel, to reach the green in two.

It was a matchless display of attacking golf, as awesome as it was daring, as aggressive as it was thrilling. His most audacious strike occurred at the sixth, where he carried the ball from the tee more than 300 yards to clear a water-filled gully guarding the green. To achieve this feat, he had to hit the ball in the direction of a television camera perched atop a large cherry-picker.

The cameraman had placed himself high enough above the course to be untroubled by anything other than low-flying aircraft – or so he thought. He had the fright of his life when Daly's drive whistled past his nose on its way to the green via the stratosphere. Watson, who has witnessed most things in his twenty-five years as a golf pro, could only shake his head and say he had never seen anything like it.

In this mood, Daly doesn't reach greens, he shells them. There are those who watch Daly swing and wonder how long it will be before he has back trouble. He turns so far and so freely, it seems more likely that one day he'll end up wearing his upper body back to front.

There is, of course, more to the man than long hitting. His short game is stylish and accomplished, and he putts well. All we can do is hope that John Daly looks after his back and his gift for some time to come. The way he plays golf is one of the great spectacles of all sport.

He won £52,000, Watson £14,000, Davies £6,500 and Senior £2,500. Davies achieved her ambition and proved her point. The organisers have invited her back next year.

On the wider issue of enhancing the situation where men and women compete together in professional tournaments, Davies was sceptical.

'Just imagine what would happen if John Daly turned up on the ladies' tour wearing a skirt,' she said.

She must stop giving Mark McCormack good ideas.

February 1996

PLAYER'S RELENTLESS DRIVE THROUGH LIFE SUSTAINED BY A TASTE OF HONEY

T HERE's not much of Gary Player (5ft 7in tall, 10st 7lb wet through) but what there is has lasted a long time and journeyed a long way. He has been a golf pro for more than forty years and in that time has travelled nine million miles.

He has the knack of turning the most gracious home into something resembling the departure lounge of a busy airport. We met in an elegant house in Ascot and picked our way to the garden over an assault course of strewn baggage. He had just returned from St Andrews, was spending a day at Wentworth raising money for charity and then going to Ireland with visits to Japan, Singapore, Jakarta, Hong Kong, China, France, Taiwan, Germany, the United States and Africa planned before the end of the year.

His business interests the world over have made him exceedingly rich without counting the millions he has made playing golf. He is guaranteed his place in the Pantheon as one of the greatest golfers of all time.

Along with Arnold Palmer and Jack Nicklaus, he built the foundation of the modern game and changed the way that golf professionals were perceived and rewarded. He is one of only four players to have won the Grand Slam of British and US Opens, the Masters and the US PGA Championship, and is the only man to have won the Open in three different decades. So why is he still charging round the world as if he was trying to make a name for himself? What makes Gary run?

'I honestly don't know. My daughter said to me the other day, "How have you lived like this for forty years? I couldn't last a week." It's not possible for anyone of my age to put in more hours than I do. I suppose part of the reason is that I came from a very poor background and that taught me not to take anything for granted. If you have nothing and then get a taste of honey, it becomes a habit.

'The other day when I was leaving home in South Africa one of my grandchildren said to me, "Why are you going away, Grandad? Come back to my house with me." I had a little weep. But how do you achieve anything without sacrifice? George Bernard Shaw said complete happiness on earth would be eternal hell and I think he's right. I've got into the routine of striving.

'But, for the first time, I'm thinking of easing up. I shall play my last Open at St Andrews in the year 2000. That's where I played my first Open in 1955 so it will be a fitting end. Then I'll retire to my stud farm and spend time with my grandchildren. Of course, I'll still continue to design golf courses and travel the world a bit,' he said. In fact, what Gary Player intends to do when he retires is just one full-time job instead of the five or six he has at present.

Player's plans have been made the more attractive by what has happened in recent years to the country of his birth. As South Africa's most famous sportsman during the time of apartheid, he became a particular target for protest. When he played the US PGA at Dayton, Ohio, in 1969 he was guarded on the course by more than fifty policemen. Three officers slept in his house at night. During the tournament protesters threw telephone directories at him as he swung, rolled golf balls on to the green as he putted and sprayed ice in his eyes as he walked from green to tee. He lost by one shot to Ray Floyd.

'It was the greatest tournament I ever played in my life,' he said.

'The athlete is not responsible for the government. I wanted to explain that I couldn't go in with a gun and

change the way things were. But now I treat all of what happened to me in that time like I do a missed putt. I don't look back.

'What I see now in my country is a bloody miracle. I really did believe that I would see snowballs in hell before I would see Nelson Mandela in a Springbok shirt being cheered by Afrikaners. Mandela is my great hero. I've been around royalty and mixed with presidents and prime ministers and the like but I have never met anyone with Mr Mandela's humility and effortless knack of doing the right thing. There is nothing false about him.

'You know the thing I'm proudest of? I never travelled on anything other than my South African passport. I could have changed but I was a South African and proud of it. I was offered a million pounds to go and live in America. I turned it down. I believed it was my job to help change what was wrong. Nowadays it amuses me when people say that a government of black men will fail. What about when the country was governed by white men? They didn't make a very good job of it, did they?'

He forks out about £500,000 a year to pay for the education of 400 black children at a school he built near his home.

'People ask me if I'll go to some godforsaken place. I don't really want to go but I tell them I will if they pay towards the school,' he said. 'It's very rewarding work. You have to imagine what it's like to see kids who live in a mud hut, who never even sat on a toilet seat, coming to school and using a computer and going to university. It's like...' He thought for a minute for a proper comparison. 'It's like winning the Open,' he said.

It says something for his resilience and self-belief that when he became the oldest man ever to make the cut at the 1995 Open, he actually thought he could win the tournament.

'I know that one day a man aged between fifty and sixty will win the Open. I lost it by three shots a round, including a 77, and I played bloody well for that 77, let me tell you.

'But what that tournament at St Andrews brought home to me was how the equipment has changed the game. Technology is making golf courses obsolete. There is no such thing as a par five. On a calm day at St Andrews, John Daly or Tiger Woods could probably drive six par fours. There are two bunkers on the ninth originally put there for the drive that nowadays players are clearing with six-irons.

'Daly is good for the game. Fine golfer. Woods has that something special. I played a round with him recently and he asked me what was wrong with his swing and I told him his swing was perfect and all he had to concentrate on was getting the attitude right. It's what goes on between the ears that makes the champion. Call it dedication, positive thinking, concentration, application or, in my case, loving adversity.'

I asked him what loving adversity meant.

'Let us say it is God's plan to sometimes give you a hard time. Why should we always assume that everything will be perfect in our life? But in adversity some people start drinking, lose confidence and disappear. The trick is to make yourself accept adversity as a part of life, like happiness. Jack Nicklaus had the best mind of anyone who ever stepped on a golf course.

'He wasn't the best striker of the ball, Weiskopf was better, so were Hogan and Sam Snead. But no one had a better mind than Nicklaus. When I first started, I was advised by one or two pros to save myself the heartache and take up another occupation. They looked at my swing and thought it unorthodox. But it's not the swing that counts.

'Look at Daly's swing. It's not possible. He's made of rubber. Look at Jack's swing – flying right elbow. Arnie's – flat. Doug Sanders – he could swing inside a telephone booth and not break a window. In the end it's all in the head.'

He should know. There have been more naturally gifted golfers, more graceful athletes, more glamorous stars than Gary Player. But few have matched his remorseless energy and immutable will. It has all, as he admits, been achieved at the expense of what the rest of us would call a normal family life. There is another ingredient which he is anxious to talk about.

'Do you know what Arnie, Jack and I have in common? Great wives. Nowadays all you hear about on the tour is divorce. The three of us have great wives. We can't claim we know how to pick 'em. Truth is, it's a miracle.'

The object of his wonderment – his wife Vivienne – was sitting in the hall surrounded by several heaps of luggage. As she surveyed the scene she shook her head and smiled ruefully.

'Here we go again,' she said.

September 1995

Gary Player gives every impression of being indestructible. His idea of easing up was to play only eighteen tournaments on the US Seniors' Tour in 1998. He had, according to a Seniors' Tour official, 'perhaps the finest season of any player over sixty years of age'. He won $450,000 in prize money. In fourteen seasons with the seniors he has won more than $6 million. He remains trim of body and mind and his enthusiasm would tire a man twenty years his junior.

TAKES MORE THAN WOODS TO RIGHT WRONGS

BEING a sporting hero never did have much to do with reality. Many have been called it but few have been able to live up to the reputation of role model. It is getting more difficult, not because standards of behaviour are worse but because media scrutiny is such even a saint would have problems surviving with reputation intact.

Seen through the prism of hero worship, the image of the sporting god has always been exaggerated, but nowadays the hero lives in an arcade of distorting mirrors. Little wonder he sometimes forgets who he is and where he came from. Tiger Woods has only just stepped into the spotlight but already he must be looking for somewhere to hide.

He is the apotheosis of the sporting hero. Once that meant children asking for his autograph and men becoming foolish in his presence. Now, it means he is the target for every crackpot, huckster and shyster in the universe.

The media froth at the mouth, agents gibber and businessmen fall over themselves to bury him in money.

In all of sport, there has never been anyone who created such a commotion. One reason is he is a very fine golfer. Some say the greatest there has ever been. We shall see. The other reason is because he is a black man playing a white man's game. From what we have seen so far, Woods is a remarkable young man possessed of art, iron will and seemingly unquenchable ambition. On the evidence of what he has so far experienced, he will need all those qualities and more if he is to achieve what is expected of him.

Ironically, he is likely to face most hostility from the race-relations sphere, organisations like the Institute of Research in African American Studies. He has already been accused of racism because he prefers to define himself as something other than a black man. In fact, if we are talking race, Tiger Woods is first and foremost a member of the human variety. Sadly, it's not as easy as that. It would be foolish to deny a black golfer did not possess a significance beyond winning trophies. On the other hand, it would be equally silly to believe the success of Woods will change the nature of prejudice existing in golf clubs, never mind the world.

When Jackie Robinson became the first black man to play major league baseball, he felt the yoke of political significance around his neck. There was no more robust adversary of racial inequality but he knew anything he might achieve would be cosmetic. Also, if he was not careful, his reputation would be used and abused by people with motives far removed from sport. In the same week that the United States celebrated the fiftieth anniversary of Robinson's achievement, it was reported that segregation in American schools was as bad now as it had been in the 1950s.

Do we honestly believe if Woods fulfils his promise and wins all of golf's prizes, the members at Augusta National will vote to allow an equal number of black golfers into the club? Don't be daft. In a racist society, the value of the black sporting hero is to persuade us to see things as they really are. For a moment, we face reality. Then we shrug and turn away.

June 1997

At the time of writing Woods is the world number one. The ratings might change but what remains constant is Tiger's reputation as the most exciting player in golf. He has star quality in abundance. Furthermore he gives every indication of treating success and failure in the same even-handed, good-natured manner. In both demeanour and attitude towards his chosen career he is the exemplary professional.

CONFESSIONS
OF AN
AMATEUR

Just Getting into the Swing of This

In the past eighteen months the family Parkinson has moved into golf in a big way. The wife, who took it up a year ago, now has more gear than Nancy Lopez. The children are practising hard in order to keep their father in some style in his later years and, as for the head of the household, well, he is at that crucial point in the life of every golfer where you either throw the clubs away or succumb to a lifetime's addiction. While he decides, the garden Chez Parkinson has undergone radical changes. The shaded part where the cat napped out of the sun is now a putting green. The cat, not being a golfer, is not surrendering his territorial rights without a fight. His first tactic was dumb insolence whereby he simply stretched out in front of a hole and had to be removed bodily and locked in the woodshed. Of late he has developed a new and sinister habit of which I will say no more than that it makes retrieving a ball with your bare hands from the hole something of an adventure.

While he balefully spectates from the woodshed window, we putt and chip the days away in search of that

elusive excellence which is the wonder drug stimulating one of the world's most spectacular growth industries. I calculate that if the greater part of this planet is water, at least two-thirds of what's left belongs to golfers. Moreover, I further calculate that if all the golf bags in Britain were dumped from the White Cliffs of Dover the United Kingdom would return to the sea from whence it came. Furthermore, if all the golfers, male and female, were laid end to end it would be, apart from a pleasurable experience, a staggering advert for gaudy leisure wear.

The impact of golf on our society has not been fully understood. For instance, the modern gurus of twentieth century society are golf pros. They have taken over from Middle European psychiatrists wearing pince nez and balding, cross-legged Indians holding joss sticks. By advising on such matters as grips and swings they cure sleeplessness, cement crumbling marriages and generally make you feel a better person. This blissful state ends as soon as you try to practise what they preach, which means you return again and again which is why, generally speaking, the golf pro is the owner of the biggest limousine in the club car park.

I have a theory about golf. It is that the game is a gigantic conspiracy involving golf pros and people who design golf courses. Everyone knows that the job of the pro is to get you to the state where you don't feel too much of a fool going out to play the course. What many people don't realise, until it is too late, is that people who design golf courses see it as their job to set the kind of problems which will have the golfer back to see his pro as soon as possible. Thus the great golfing conspiracy, with designers and pros bouncing the poor player between them like some hapless shuttlecock.

I would add that some caddies of my acquaintance are part of the conspiracy. Someone once described humour as being the difference between man's aspiration and his achievements. Nowhere is the truth of this observation more apparent than on a golf course, which is why caddies are people who have learned to keep a straight face while observing one of life's great comedies. If they fell about laughing at the antics of their employer they would soon be seeking alternative employment. Instead, they remain straight-faced until, on the back nine, they single out the odd good shot for comment and praise. It's not the shot that brings you back, it's what the caddie says about it that matters.

Mind you, having said that, I would hate caddies to think I have cast them as humourless people. The opposite is true. A lifetime spent observing the human race at its most absurd has given most of them a deft line in dry humour. A friend of mine, a notoriously bad-tempered player, was coming down the homeward straight after a round which had sorely tried his self-control. Playing his approach shot for the final green he landed deep in a bunker. At this he went berserk and, after trying to break his club over his knee (a singularly futile and painful pastime), he hurled the wretched iron far into a clump of dense bracken. There was a silence, broken only by the sound of my friend's heavy breathing and the voice of his caddie who whispered into his left earhole, 'If I were you, sir, I'd take an optional club.'

Funny people golfers, but not half so funny as the people who observe them.

July 1980

Voyaging into the Unknown

Playing in your first pro-celebrity golf match is a voyage into the unknown like marriage or eating haggis or entering a ferret legging* competition for the first time. In other words, you start by anticipating the best and end up with a ferret in your underpants.

I speak from raw and bitter experience. When the invitation arrived to play four days in a pro-celebrity tournament on a championship course in the Home Counties, I should have thrown the letter in the fire. Instead, I accepted, intoxicated by the flattery of the invitation, giddy with the innocence of one new to the game.

In truth, I was a lamb to the slaughter because it was

---

* Ferret legging – Britain's fastest growing sport. It has the virtue of being utterly simple. The participant puts a ferret down his trousers having first secured the trouser bottom with string. The winner is the one who lasts longest. The present world champions is Reg Mellor, of Barnsley, who once had a ferret in his trousers for six hours. So far there are no plans for a Pro-Celebrity Ferret Legging competition.

only twelve months ago – and then reluctantly – that I had approached golf in a serious manner. Indeed, it is not too long ago that, as President of the Anti-Golf Society, I was about as welcome at the nation's golf courses as a family of moles or an acute case of turf rot.

What happened to change my life was simply that my friends deserted me, seduced by the blasted game.

Twelve months after disbanding my society, I was playing with a handicap of 20 and in the mood to try the world of pro-celebrity. Now generally speaking, pro-celebrity golf is what it says it is, celebrities and professionals, playing together along with any amateur who will pay a few grand to charity to join them. Normally it is a relaxing and jolly day.

Unwittingly, I picked the one golf bun-fight which mattered, in that the professionals in the tournament I played in were competing for £150,000 in prize money and Ryder Cup points. It proved to be as relaxing and jolly as the battle of Monte Cassino.

Looking back, I should have retired after the very first day, nay even the first hole, because in truth it was blindingly obvious from the beginning that the entire enterprise was going to be a dreadful ordeal. At the first tee there were a good few hundred people to see us on our way. My three playing partners went ahead of me and drove the ball up the fairway in the approved manner.

I chose an alternative method. Using my three-wood I contrived to hit the ball on its head so that it buried the tee and rolled forward all of six inches. The crowd stood in horrified silence, my playing partners shuffled uncomfortably like people who see a drunken friend try to shake hands with a hat stand. The silence was cracked by my caddie who said in stage whisper, 'Look on the bright side. It only went six inches but it was dead on target.'

Two shots later I was away from the shame on the tee and decently buried in a wooded grove where I could contemplate in private my next shot and folly. I decided on a pitching wedge to the green, visualising as I studied what lay ahead, both the shot and my triumphant walk to the green. As I picked up the club in my backswing, a voice behind me said very clearly, 'I say, they're waiting for you on the green.'

I froze in the swing and swivelled to see a man carrying a bag of sandwiches and a flask of tea standing behind me. He was beaming.

'What did you say?' I queried.

'I said that they are waiting for you up on the green,' he said, beaming.

'How would you like this pitching wedge wrapped round your neck?' I asked.

'I'd report you to the PGA for ungentlemanly conduct,' he replied.

'You might find it difficult with this club down our throat,' I said.

Now, such exchanges, though dramatic, are no part of a game of golf. Nor do they help the mug golfer settle down and concentrate. The consequence of my rancorous encounter with the spectator was that my round, which from the start had the quality of a bad dream, became a Technicolor nightmare. My new-found friend, still clutching tea flask and sandwiches – a clear sign he was not leaving in a hurry – followed me for ten holes, standing in my eye-line whenever he could, a mute and glowering testament to my folly.

During that first round and through the ensuing three days my caddie found my golf distinctly humorous. His lack of faith in my ability was obvious and at every tee shot when the other caddies would await their players' putt by positioning themselves 200 yards or so down the fairway, he would hide behind the nearest tree. This ploy did nothing for my confidence and caused mild panic among spectators who were quite rightly concerned that, if I terrified my caddie, I might do them a terrible mischief.

He was unremitting in his attitude. Once when I played an exquisite chip to within a foot of the flag, he dropped to the ground in a mock faint. Again, when I hit an eight-iron out of a bunker on to the green, a shot even my pro saluted, my caddie was unimpressed. As he handed me the putter he said, 'You lucky sod.'

In the clubhouse, friends consoled me with stories of what had befallen other celebrities in similar tournaments. Their kindness was tempered by the realisation that a catalogue of my disasters would shortly be used to persuade some other unfortunate debutant. The story would, no doubt, begin, 'If you think you are bad you should see Mike Parkinson play.'

To be fair, I did gain quite a bit from the experience. I established for certain that the life of a professional golfer is more arduous than glamorous and that the game they play is, along with cricket, one of the most difficult and complex of all. Moreover, the entire operation proved to me once and for all that middle age is when you realise that your sporting fantasies are not just unattainable but simply ludicrous even to contemplate.

But the final comment was delivered by a young fan who approached me on the last day with her autograph book. She asked politely for my signature and then busied herself finding an appropriate page. She flicked over the section marked 'golf professionals', to which I could have no objection, but also passed through the section marked 'celebrities', which worried me slightly. In the end she found what she was looking for. My appropriate section. She handed me the book. The page was headed 'miscellaneous'. Out of the mouth of babes and sucklings...

September 1985

Reluctant Convert to Hacking

It was in Spain that my reluctant conversion to golf began. My teacher was Mr James Tarbuck, a passionate advocate of the game and a very fine player. Firstly he invited me to walk with him while he played a match against Norman Hunter, the soccer player.

Those fortunate enough to have watched Mr Hunter play soccer will know that he did not take prisoners. Sadly, he was born before his time, for he was surely put on earth to sort out the likes of Maradona. The 'Hand of God' would have counted for nothing when it came up against 'God's Clog'.

The power of Norman Hunter's left peg was in evidence on the golf course when, after missing a short putt on the eighteenth and losing to Jimmy, he gave his putter a ferocious kick. As it spiralled spectacularly skywards, glinting in the Iberian sun, Jimmy said to him, 'Norman, the caddie has just recognised you.'

Shortly after this, Jimmy arranged my inaugural round. At the third hole he suggested I drive first and showed me the line. The shot looked difficult and dangerous because it involved driving over the top of a group of workmen.

'Shout fore,' said Jimmy. I did and was perturbed to see the men return my warning with what I took to be offensive gestures.

'Tell them to sod off,' said my friend. So I did and they retreated, shaking their fists.

I settled down and hit the shot in the direction specified by my partner. I looked to him for praise.

'Good shot,' he said, 'except that the hole is down there,' pointing in the opposite direction.

The most humiliating part was retrieving my ball watched by the workmen I had so abused and who were not used to seeing their course played that way.

That I survived the ordeal and have arrived at my present state where I have dedicated my remaining years to the search for the perfect swing is a clear indication of golf's allure.

I am now a regular on the pro-celebrity circuit, where I am known as 'Awesome' Parkinson. This identity was bestowed upon me by Rodger Davis during a round we played together some time ago. Mr Davis chose the word carefully after observing my game for several holes. What convinced him was an eight-iron to the green which he suggested I should float on the breeze. What happened was I thinned the shot and the ball nearly knee-capped a spectator, took the top from a grassy knoll, hit a tree and came to rest four feet from the flag. Mr Davis regarded the carnage and shook his head. 'Awesome' is what he said, and that is what I am called.

Pro-celebrity golf divides opinion. There are those who believe it is worth any amount of public humiliation just for the joy of playing a round with a great golfer. These are called Celebrities. Then there are those who take part only because they have to and who spend the entire round trying to avoid contact with their partner's swing just in case it is contagious. These are called Professionals.

The fact is that any joy there might be in a pro-celebrity game belongs exclusively to those of us who are lucky enough to march down the fairway with our heroes and pretend it is the last day of the Open and all we need is a birdie to take the trophy.

I have indulged that particular fantasy with the likes of Nick Faldo, Gary Player, Lee Trevino, Ronan Rafferty, Tony Jacklin, Neil Coles, Howard Clark, Rodger Davis and Ian Baker-Finch, to mention but a few.

All you learn is that you will never hit the ball like them even if you lived to be a hundred. What you envy is their rhythm, what you admire is their respect for the etiquette of the game and their patience with the hackers.

More than any other group of sportsmen, professional golfers are continually pestered by amateurs in search of a cure for a hook or a slice or, worst of all (and don't even say it, just spell it out) a s-h-a-n-k.

My approach is a little more subtle. I let them drink in my swing until they feel obliged to comment. They always do and none of it has been complimentary.

July 1990

Problems of a
Below-Par Partner

WHENEVER anyone asks me how I became interested in golf I blame the wife. She showed me how.

Her enthusiasms were intoxicating her powers of persuasion overwhelming. There was a struggle. For a short period of time I became a Slob Golfer. This involved a reluctant interest in the game best defined as a cut-price protest. I played golf, but I refused to be seduced by its merchandising.

Thus I found a disgraceful bag and filled it with rusty clubs and second-hand balls. I played in a pair of modified cricket boots, old corduroys and a flat cap someone left at our house years ago. This ludicrous protest came to an end when, while playing my wife, I was approached by a man walking his dog on the course.

He watched Mary tee off and said, 'That's a lovely swing.' I agreed. He looked me up and down. 'You her caddy?' he enquired.

Nowadays what you see when I step from the clubhouse is someone who blends into the golfing landscape, a man born to stride the fairways with a fair degree of

confidence and style. This transformation is almost entirely due to the wife.

I wanted to be as happy as she is on a golf course and though I will never reach that state of nirvana, I am now at a stage where, generally speaking, the game improves my humour instead of ruining it.

I have a theory that women enjoy golf best of all because they see it primarily as a soothing pastime, whereas men mostly regard it as a test of aggression and strength. The fact is golf requires more of what are regarded as feminine qualities than almost any other sport I can think of.

It is a game requiring hands that are 'soft', swings that

are smooth. It best responds to gentle rhythms. It is about persuasion rather than power. It better suits the subtle patience of women than the brusque temperament of men.

You will realise, I hope, that I have just defined the difference between me and the wife. It took me some time to realise that it was because of those differences that she was the better golfer. Perhaps men are also more stupid than women?

How else can I explain the times I tried to blast the ball from the tee instead of following her example of a relaxed and easy swing? Why did I take a three-iron and end up in the water when she had already showed me that a five-iron, a wedge and a putt was the sensible way to play the hole?

Why did I throw clubs and curse and grind my teeth while she would dismiss disappointment with a shrug of the shoulders? Why did she look at me piteously when I wanted to abuse the slow fourball ahead or fight the galloping twoball for driving into us?

Why is she a better golfer than I am? See above. The problem is getting rid of all those years of male conditioning. The frustrations men suffer on a golf course are not because they are playing badly but because they cannot solve problems with brute strength. I have been fortunate in that my two golfing mentors have been Mary and Lozza, a piano player by profession, who knows all about what I would call the adagio approach to golf.

It was Lozza who taught me the musical accompaniment to the golf swing designed to give it the correct speed and rhythm. This involves swinging the club to the opening bars of 'The Blue Danube'.

If you imagine the music as 'Da, dee, da, daaa...dum' then the club should be taken back to 'Da, dee, da'. By the next 'daa' it should be at the top of the backswing and starting the descent and the final 'dum' is the club head striking the ball and the follow through.

It works; or at least it sets the swing to waltz time which, when you think about it, is about right. Try it. Humming is perfectly acceptable if you are unable to play the tune in your head. Whistling is not recommended because it sounds common and interferes with your breathing.

Other musical tips include using the song 'Blue Moon' as an aid to putting. If you sing the first two words of the song as a ballad and take the putter head back on 'Blue' and through on 'Moon' you will do wonders for your game. If you need further guidance on the correct tempo, I suggest Ella Fitzgerald's version on 'The Rodgers and Hart Songbook' has it about right whereas Sinatra's on 'Swingin' Session' is not quite right, despite having the better title for a golfer seeking inspiration.

Similarly, both Lozza and I are convinced that the correct choice of music as you drive to the club is as important a part of preparation as half an hour spent chipping and putting. I find Johnny Hodges playing the blues and Ben Webster at his most languid ideal for the purpose.

The worst I ever saw Lozza play was when he arrived in a car driven by a friend who played a tape of 'The

Flight of The Bumble Bee' performed on a xylophone.

At no time are the soothing effects of music needed more than when a man plays his wife. People flogging pension funds and retirement villas in Portugal paint an idyllic picture of you and the missus spending a golden twilight together, walking down life's fairway towards the Great Clubhouse In The Sky. The message is that having worked together for so long you can now relax and see out the rest of your life as golfing partners.

I don't know what the figures are but my guess would be that this kind of selling has led to a sharp increase in the divorce rate among the over-sixties. I recommend any couple thinking of getting married to play a round of golf together first. Unlike sleeping together before marriage, a pre-nuptial round of golf will give the woman the clearest indication possible of what life with him will really be like.

It takes a great deal of patience, fortitude, good humour and forgiveness if a married couple are to become golfing partners. There are fundamental differences and they must be addressed.

Take, for instance, the bag. In the main, women (meaning my wife) prepare their golf bag bearing in mind the possibility that while they are playing the fourteenth hole World War III will be declared and we will spend at least twelve months living in a bunker.

Therefore, in addition to a full set of clubs, my wife's bag contains a survival kit of sweets and various nibbles, a flask of tea, bottles of mineral water, insect repellents, sun creams and a tin of Elastoplast. She will also have packed various articles of tropical clothing as well as thermal underwear, thick sweaters and a complete set of waterproofs in case she has to be rescued by the Felixstowe lifeboat.

I am nowhere near as organised, or prepared. My problem is that my sons nick my golf equipment and I have to take what's left.

What is funny is when we go to play charity pro-ams together and the caddies see us coming. They jostle for Mary's attention figuring she'll have the smaller carry. They can't believe what they see when I point her bag out to them.

She loves pro-ams whereas I approach them as I would a rabid dog. The problem is they always play Mary in front of me so that throughout my round I am constantly being informed that the hole I just three-putted was birdied by my wife fifteen minutes before.

It is even worse when they put us together in the same match. Pros love playing with Mary because she's always on the cut stuff and using her shots to get pars while they shoot for the birdies. Playing with me is a bit like going on a wildlife safari.

Moreover, when they look at her set-up and her swing they realise they have something to work with if she seeks advice. By comparison I represent a lost cause.

Once we played at Turnberry with Gary Player and his wife. We swapped partners for the encounter. Mary went into one of these impossible pot bunkers and couldn't get out. Mr Player showed her how and she hit the ball to within two feet of the pin.

Soon after, I went into a similar bunker. I looked around for help. My three playing partners were looking out to sea. They thought they were being kind.

If we were to tally up the many games we have played against each other, I would guess that the wife holds a substantial lead. However, there are signs that I am catching up.

It's not simply that I'm becoming a more canny golfer so much as I've learned to understand that defeat doesn't mean I have lost to a mere woman, rather I have been beaten by a better golfer.

I will not pretend our golfing relationship is perfect. It is generally true that if you see us walking together down the fairway you can assume that I am in the lead whereas if you see me trailing five yards behind looking hang-dog it's a fair chance I am three down with four to play.

There are still moments when defeat is hard to accept without rancour. Like the other day when she rolled one in from fifteen feet to win on the last. I was choked and she knew it. She picked the ball from the hole and said sweetly, 'You know, there are times when I'd hate to be playing against me.'

I am still trying to compose the musical antidote to that one.

April 1991

Pressure is When Your Team are Banking on You

I HAVE always been sceptical of the so-called pressures of modern sport. I think pressure is being unemployed or homeless, not getting up in the morning and having no greater worry than playing a round of golf for a living or kicking a football for ten grand a week. But I must admit that when Herr Langer stood over that putt on the eighteenth to settle the Ryder Cup, I was hiding behind our settee with my hands over my eyes. The wife had to go for a lie-down and she's not been the same woman since. It has affected her golf (more of that later). I think she's in mourning.

What the last act of the drama at Kiawah Island demonstrated to all of us, particularly the players, was that pressure is not, as is commonly supposed, about missing a putt if you've already been paid $50,000 just to turn up, and know that, in any case, there's a couple of million in the bank. What it showed is it really matters when you are putting to decide the fate of your team and their supporters.

Pressure is When Your Team

I had a similar moment playing at Collingtree Park near Northampton, in a fourball competition for the Variety Club. I must say I played the front nine to my great satisfaction, scoring 23 Stableford points. Our team total was 46 and as we came to the turn we were in the lead and good heart.

Our trouble started on the eleventh when, with two of our team losing balls in the lake, our fourball reached the green with a combined total of 22 shots. When I tell you I was in a greenside bunker for two, you will understand what a terrible struggle my team-mates had to get the ball somewhere near the flag. I was the hope of my side. If I could get up and down in two we would have three points and at least maintain our momentum.

I opened my stance just like Jose Maria and imagined the commentary by Alliss: 'This is where he reaps the dividend of all those lonely hours of practice...' I took

what I imagined to be a long slow swing, aiming two inches behind the ball and sent it hurtling out of the bunker, one bounce into the bunker opposite.

Never mind. Get it out, sink the putt and we still have two points. Forget Jose Maria. He never could play anyway. This time you are Nick and you want a high stopper. The ball is sitting up in the bunker and there's about twenty feet to the pin. Close the face a bit, break the wrists quickly, get it up and out. Just like the video. In the video the ball lobs out of the bunker and stops six inches from the flag. In real life it rose vertically from the depths like a dolphin at feeding time and plonked deep into the front fringe of the bunker.

Think positively. Chip it out and in and we still have one point.

My problem was that there is no coaching manual I know of, no video I have seen, which shows you how to play a chip with one foot in a deep bunker and the other leg atop. At a rough guess, the shot would be best attempted by a man with one leg four feet longer than the other. As it was, I attempted to play the ball by standing in the bunker with my back to the hole, trying to hit the ball with what can only be described as a paddling shot. I looked like a man escaping down river in a canoe.

It says much for the strength and resilience of my team that our challenge did not crumple at this point. In fact, we rallied and as we came to the last hole, we were in a situation where six points would make the difference between winning a bronze figurine of a man lining up a putt, or an umbrella.

Now the eighteenth at Collingtree is worthy of careful explanation because it is one of the most demanding finishing holes I have come across.

It is a par five requiring a cautious drive alongside a lake and a carefully judged second shot into an area bounded by bunkers and water to face the challenge of a moated green. With a drive, a six-iron and a seven-iron I was on the green in regulation and thinking of turning pro. I was twenty feet from the flag. From a distance it looked a certain five.

It was not until I reached the green that I realised the designer had decided to have the last laugh. He had sloped the green left to right towards the water and filled it with secret gullies and hidden undulations.

I looked at the putt for a long time and didn't have an idea where the ball was going. I took four putts to get down and even now I couldn't tell you how I got the ball in the hole.

My only consolation is the certain knowledge that better players than I will do the same, and worse, in the future. That is the joy of golf: the understanding that no matter how badly you play there is someone, somewhere, having an even more desperate time. That very evening, watching the telly from behind the furniture, I knew for a certain fact that Bernhard Langer would have swapped his five at Kiawah Island for my seven at Collingtree Park.

I don't know how Bernhard went about his rehabilitation, but I settled for a round of golf with the wife at

Wentworth. We played the Edinburgh course, which is as tough to play as it is beautiful to behold.

The first hole gives a fair indication of what you are in for. From a raised tee you have a fair chance of seeing the flag on the green if you are blessed with perfect eyesight, the weather is crystal clear and you are using a Field Marshal's binoculars. It leads you into hitherto unexplored areas of Wentworth estate, some so remote and private they are worthy of a visit by David Attenborough.

The virtue of playing with the wife is that you can have a row without ruining a beautiful friendship. The fact is we were both a bit testy because of losing the Ryder Cup to the Yanks and also having been behind a Japanese fourball at Gleneagles the week before. Both experiences had taken a lot out of us.

What I cannot understand is the discrepancy between the acknowledged efficiency of the Japanese in business matters and their inability to play a round of golf in less time than it takes to make several hundred motor cars. This question needs urgently addressing if we are not to reach a situation where golf on British courses will have to be conducted under supervision of a United Nations peacekeeping force.

All this is by way of explaining that we were not in the best of moods to tackle the problems set by a course as testing as the Edinburgh. We decided to walk off at the thirteenth, but we had little idea of where we were in relation to the clubhouse. I set off in the lead, partly because I wasn't talking to the wife but mainly because I am the acknowledged pathfinder in the family. We reached a crossroads.

'Left,' I said.

'Straight ahead,' said the wife. This is a woman who has to be given a road map to get to the local shops. I ignored her and forked left. She followed, muttering. We had been walking for twenty minutes when I began to think something was wrong. We came to another cross roads.

'Straight on,' I said.

'Right,' said the wife, her voice becoming enfeebled by fatigue. I saw a clearing ahead and heard the sound of traffic. We headed towards it like thirsty souls seeing an oasis, which is how we came to be standing on the A30 somewhere between the Chertsey turn-off and Chiquito's Mexican restaurant, fully dressed for a round of golf and pulling large bags on trolleys.

We were not, it must be said, the kind of people you normally find hitch-hiking on a dual carriageway. Several cars slowed down to have a look at us as if we were Martians newly landed. One young man recognised me and shouted, 'I didn't know you could hit 'em this far, Parky.' I waved in nonchalant manner pretending I was going to a fancy-dress party, while the wife muttered something behind me which sounded like 'You prat'.

We made it back to the clubhouse about an hour later. Bernard Gallacher, lately arrived back from Kiawah Island, was outside the pro's shop. He too had suffered a hard day.

'You are not going to tell me you could have sunk the

putt that Bernhard missed?' he said. I shook my head. It wasn't that I didn't have an opinion. I was simply too knackered to speak.

What I wanted to say was that no matter how long they play, the pros will never know the real problems faced every day by thousands of ordinary golfers.

Like I've always said: they don't know what real pressure is.

October 1991

GOLFERS IN THE SWING

PORTUGAL was stirring from hibernation. The sun shone every day, gently thawing out winter bones, and when the cloud came it was as flimsy as a bride's veil.

It was perfect weather for The Jimmy Tarbuck Golf Classic, which this year took place on the San Lorenzo course in the Algarve and in several karaoke bars.

At the end of the week it was demonstrable that those who had spent most time practising karaoke did not return the best scores. On the other hand, they looked like they had had a good time, which is more than can be said for one or two of the prizewinners who appeared to require the services of a counsellor in post-competition stress.

The fact is that while most of us might entertain thoughts of emulating our heroes and playing golf for a living, few of us realise how tiring it is pretending to be a professional golfer. The strain showed on our foursome fairly early in the week when High Handicapper asked our captain what he should do.

Without inspecting the predicament, our captain said through clenched teeth, 'Hit the ball as hard as you can, as far as you can – and as quickly as you can.'

Not being a sensitive fellow, High Handicapper took our captain at his word and almost swung himself off his feet in an effort to follow instructions. The outcome was the most dreadful slice into a pine forest. We trooped in search, moving slowly like mourners, faces set grim.

Looking at us you would not have imagined we were on holiday and having a lovely time. When we found the ball it was behind a tree, lying against a root, as safe from human hand as a fox in its lair.

We looked at the disaster. High Handicapper said, 'What shall I do?' Only a vein throbbing in our captain's forehead showed how fiercely he fought to retain self-control.

Looking his team-mate in the eye, he said, 'Well it seems to me you have two options. One is you can find a phone box, look through Yellow Pages and find a lumberjack. Then you could call him and ask him to

come down here with his equipment and chop down yonder pine.

'If, in the meantime, he could also dig up the root without moving your ball you might conceivably be able to chip out on to the fairway. Failing that, you could pick up and leave the scoring on this hole to the rest of us in which case we might get back to the clubhouse before the holiday is over.'

High Handicapper considered these options for a moment and then said, 'I think I'd better pick up.'

Golf gives wonderful insights into the human psyche. By narrowing our ambitions to the seemingly simple proposition of getting a ball into a small hole in the ground, it reveals the basic man. Our High Handicapper is a discernible type, familiar to anyone who has ever played a round of golf. He always asks the most obvious questions. My theory is that when he asks, 'What shall I do?' when the answer is plain, he is merely transferring responsibility to his playing partner.

If he messes up your instructions he gives you a dirty look and tells them in the clubhouse you cost him the hole. If the shot comes off he will walk away in triumph as if it was always his own idea.

These players are also the ones who have a complete lexicon of drivel to accompany every bad shot. They hook the ball off the tee and, as it screams towards the tree-line, shout 'Catch the wind' or 'Fade' as if there was a master plan attached to their incompetence.

My favourite is the badly aimed shot going seventy yards wide of the target accompanied by this commentary from the striker: 'Turn...why doesn't it turn? Just look at it going straight on. Keep left. Where's the wind? Come on, wind. Bend on the wind, ball. Come left.' Inevitably the ball ignores these instructions and disappears into the undergrowth whereupon the golfer turns to his companions and says, 'Would you believe it?'

These are the players who never get a good lie on the fairway, who are always in bunkers that have been robbed of sand and who have never had a putt which wasn't sabotaged by a sprig mark or a hidden borrow. If golf is a test of character it is not because of the game itself but the company we keep.

Needless to say our team did not feature among the prizewinners. Our triumph was that we finished still speaking to one another. The real bonus of the trip was the discovery of a wonderful golf course. San Lorenzo is not the longest golf course in Europe but it's one of the toughest.

It has a beguiling start, par five, par three and two par fours, one dog-leg left, the other dog-leg right. Nothing too tough and you feel quite pleased with yourself as you reach the high ground and come in view of the Atlantic.

What faces you is one of those awkward par threes, 130 yards across a chasm to the green, stroke index 17. It is when you move to the next tee that the real test begins.

From the sixth tee you can see a lot of the Atlantic Ocean and not much of the fairway, which follows the contours of the coastline turning left towards the green. The prevailing wind is off the sea and into your face.

The next hole similarly hugs the coastline while the

eighth is one of the most difficult par fives you will every play. To start with it is 570 yards long. It turns inland but towards more water in the form of a large lake. The green itself is reached across water and the landing area looks as narrow as a surfboard.

The back nine are even more spectacular than the front with pine trees and flowering almond blossom and views of distant hills the colour and shape of sleeping elephants.

The finishing hole is one of the most spectacular I have ever played. The drive skirts a lake, the second shot is across another lake to a green surrounded by bunkers. On the other hand, if you are either very brave or extremely foolhardy you could try to drive across the lake towards the green from the tee. You had better be able to hit the driver in excess of 270 yards otherwise you are in trouble.

I have described the course because it is worth remarking on, but also to give you the setting for one of the most remarkable comebacks ever seen in modern golf. I am talking about the match between myself and my partner, Irish Joe the Pro, and the two lads who own the karaoke club, John and Jeremy.

They were big lads and gave the ball a terrible spank. Joe is not short off the tee either, in fact he's a long hitter for a man about to collect his bus pass. His real talent is that he's an Irish golfer, which is to say a conjuror of shots, as adept with the back of a club as the face of it.

We started quite well by halving the first hole. However, when we came to the sixth with the sun sparkling off the Atlantic and the seabirds wheeling, we were four down.

'What do we do partner?' I asked Joe.

'Nivver fear. This is where the course begins and where superior tactics will decide the match,' said my partner.

At that precise moment, Jeremy hit a drive which started off towards America, swung left along the edge of the sea and landed on the centre of the fairway a nine-iron from the green; which is how it came to pass that with six holes played we were five down.

'Things are desperate,' I said to my partner. Whereupon he came out with one of the great lines in modern sport.

'Just let's keep playing the way we are,' he said. Only an Irishman could say such a thing and mean it.

'Joe, if we keep on playing the way we are, I said, 'we will be finished after the eleventh hole.'

His optimism reminded me of Matt Busby's memorable advice to his team in the semi-final of the European Cup in Madrid when they were two down at half-time and, to all intents and purposes, finished. He put his head round the dressing-room door, contemplated the scene of abject misery and said: 'All right lads. Just keep on playing fitba'.'

It was also reminiscent in its sanguine approach to impending disaster of the moment when Graham Stevenson, the Yorkshire cricketer, walked to the wicket for England at Sydney last man in with 20 needed to win.

There were 50,000 Australians baying for blood around the ground and in the middle a welcoming committee of more Australians who wasted little time in informing Stevenson that he was an unwelcome Pom and illegitimate to boot.

He was greeted by his fellow Yorkshireman David Bairstow, who said to him, by way of an invitation to a tactical discussion: 'What tha' reckon then, Stevo?' Whereupon his friend surveyed the scene, the lights, the noise, the insults and the scoreboard showing they needed to score 20 to win the match for their country and said: 'It's nice out here, innit?'

It must be said that my partner didn't exactly follow his own advice. He started playing much better so that we reached the tenth only three down.

The turning point on the back nine came when our opponents drove into the pines and instead of playing out elected to go for the green through the kind of forest thick enough to hide a squadron of tanks. They more or less hit out simultaneously, one shot sounding like the echo of the other.

Standing on the fairway with Joe, I witnessed the most extraordinary sight. As the balls ricocheted around the pines, trimming branches and lopping tops, so the natural inhabitants of the wood took flight. The air was thick with fleeing birds, furry animals broke cover and ran for their lives across the fairway. It looked like the scene from 'Bambi' when the hunters comb the woods.

'I've nivver seen anythin' like that,' said the Irishman, preparing to win the hole unhindered by opponents.

As we walked off the green, there were carrion birds

circling the forest inspecting the debris for casualties. We won the next two holes and halved the match.

Funny game golf – and unpredictable too – thank the Lord!

February 1992

Rattled by a Trolley
While the Wife Made
Light of her Load

IT WAS a spiffing day for golf. The sun shone with some warmth, the breeze was a baby's breath and Wentworth was looking as fresh as a spring bride. If you haven't played the opening hole on the Edinburgh course then try to arrange to do so before you die. It's a long par four, 458 yards, which you contemplate from a raised tee.

What you see are bunkers guarding the left-hand side of the fairway and beyond them a drop on to the rough at the eighteenth hole. The fairway nudges right and the green, large and inviting, is the sort you would never suspect of treachery until you find yourself above the hole when, with the surface shiny, you would settle for a three putt.

I scrambled a five, which put me in good heart. I have been known to spend days on that green. The wife made a four. I don't know why I bother. It was a long and tiring round, mainly because it is a long and tiring golf course, and when we came to the eighteenth we were properly pooped.

This is some finishing hole, a 472 yard par four with tight out of bounds on the right, a narrow fairway and a collar of rough in front of the green just in case you might think of scuttling a shot to the flag.

I settled for a six. So did Mary. I was so overcome at having halved a hole with the wife that I volunteered to pull her trolley, as well as my own, up the steep hill to the clubhouse.

It is the sort of gesture made by lovesick swains in the first flush of pubescent ardour – showing off. It is not to be recommended for a middle-aged man with a bad back, particularly one married to a woman who owns the biggest golf bag in the world. I have seen professional caddies swoon away and feign illness when approached by my wife to carry her bag.

Lugging the two bags behind me, I set off up the hill at a gallop. Two days later when I couldn't get out of bed, I realised what a silly old fool I had been. I am typing this with my neck in a collar, living on painkillers and manipulation.

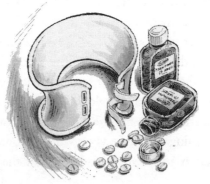

What you discover when you damage your neck and back is that every golfer you meet has suffered in a similar fashion. What is more, they all know someone in Goole, Basingstoke or Margate who is a genius at cracking backs.

I am being treated by a doctor who is also a member of Wentworth golf club. When we got the X-rays, I asked him what he thought.

'The neck is pretty ropey,' he said. I am 5–4 against watching the Masters on television, never mind playing in it.

Personally, I blame those dratted trolleys. Hauling them around golf courses can't do any good at all. I don't know if there has been any research done into the damage they cause to the human frame but I am willing to give evidence.

In future I am going to carry. It means fewer clubs but why do we need all that metal in any case? Playing with half a set and carrying when the winter restrictions were applied at the club, I found I played just as badly as I always do and finished the round feeling frisky.

What is more, with everyone carrying, it was a discernibly quicker game of golf. However, I must tell you that the wife is the only person I know whose light carry bag is bigger than her normal tournament job.

She makes nothing of her load, shrugging it on her shoulder and striding round the course like a twenty year old. It is one thing to realise your wife is a better golfer, quite another to admit she's also stronger than you.

April 1993

THE MAGIC MAY FADE,
BUT THE DRAW REMAINS

'THE MAGIC'S gone,' said the wife.
    'If this is the parting of the ways, can I have custody of the Wisdens?' I said.

'I'm not talking about our marriage, you twerp. The magic has gone from my golf,' she said.

I said I was relieved, although it didn't take me long to work out that a divorce would be considerably cheaper than my wife's continued search for perfection on the golf course. She has propped up the economy of several countries by her generous and dedicated support of local golf professionals and throughout the world there are teachers and caddies whose eyes light up when they hear Mrs Parkinson is on the way to pay a visit.

If she asked me what's wrong – which she never does – I would have to tell her that I think she is confused. She has been taught so many different techniques that her mind is in a turmoil at address.

She will try anything. In Australia, I found her on a practice range with her upper arms pinioned by a webbing strap and a medicine ball between her knees.

I should say that the pro was similarly constrained and

both were practising a method devised by Mr Leadbetter in America. Or so they said.

Whatever they were doing, it didn't look like a lot of fun, so I didn't pursue the matter further.

There was, however, one occasion when I thought things had gone too far. The problem is that my wife is a warm and friendly soul who has never yet met a golf pro she didn't want to adopt. She was particularly pleased by a pro in Spain whom, she felt, understood her game and made her play better.

One day when I went to pick her up from her lesson, I saw the pro lifting his shirt and the wife staring intently at what was on view.

'What on earth is going on?' I asked, sounding like the affronted husband. 'Juan is showing me his operation scars', she said.

It is sad when someone who has such dedication and love for golf becomes depressed by it. So when the wife announced that the magic had departed her game I broke

the rule of a lifetime and said I would play a round of winter golf. My attitude to winter golf is cautious. I see no sense in dressing up like a lighthouse keeper to play a round of golf. Normally I am seen on a course between December and March only in exceptional circumstances.

I came to this decision after playing Gleneagles on a wincingly cold day. I remember because I was wearing ladies' tights for the first time. They are far and away the most efficient and comfortable means of keeping your legs warm but putting them on in the locker room is not advised in areas unaccustomed to the modern trend of what is known in some quarters as bi-fashion and others as cross-dressing.

The other problem with wearing tights is how the wearer would face the crisis of being taken ill on the course and having to explain to the ambulance man how he came to be wearing a pair of ladies' 15-denier panty-hose.

I do not know what my partner at Gleneagles was wearing under his trousers but he had on his head the most remarkable hat I have ever seen. Constructed of wool and waterproof plastic it had a flap to stop the water running down his neck. There was a large peak at the front to keep the water from his eyes and earflaps which he strapped to the side of his face by tying the end under his chin. He looked like a survivor of the retreat from Leningrad.

When we reached the highest part of the course he stood on the tee and looked around him. His eyes were running, two candles fell from his nose, there was frost on his eyebrows and his lips were cracked and chapped.

And do you know what he said to me? 'It's a beautiful game, golf, isn't it?' And he meant it.

Since then I have been careful about playing golf in the winter, but clearly the crisis in the wife's life took precedence over my ambition never to be cold on a golf course again.

So off we went to regain the magic. I teed off, walked over to my wife on the ladies' tee and together we strolled down the first. I found my ball and was surprised I couldn't see the wife's ball on the fairway since the last time she missed the cut stuff, Jim Callaghan was the Prime Minister. We searched for her ball, she moaning the while that this was certain proof the magic had gone forever and me nearly believing her.

We were joined by two greenkeepers and then by a friendly fourball making their way back to the clubhouse. There were now eight of us engaged in trying to find the wife's ball. We must have looked like a line of volunteers helping the police in an inch-by-inch search for clues.

Finally I said to her, 'Think back to the tee. What sort of shot did you play? Did you hit it well?'

The search stopped as she pondered the question. Our future strategy depended upon her reply.

'Oh, my God,' she said.

'What is it?' I cried.

'I didn't hit the ball at all,' she said.

'You missed it?' I said.

'No, I forgot to take the drive,' she said.

Later, in the clubhouse, the general consensus was that

they had never heard anything like it. We could all tell stories of drives that ended up in trees, or down a rabbit hole or in the back of a passing lorry. I once drove the ball in the opposite direction to the fairway, having been given the line by a partner with a suspect sense of humour. But none of us could recall an instance when the player forgot to take a shot.

It has to be reported that the wife made light of her forgetfulness. By the time we reached the sixteenth I was three down with three to play, which is the way it has always been and no doubt ever will be. She won the game on the eighteenth by chipping in for a birdie.

'Magic,' I said. She gave me an old-fashioned look.

Providing she remembers in future to take every shot, I can see little wrong with her game. Mind you, I'm the last person you should ask about magic. If you've never had it, how do you know what you are looking for?

December 1991

Black Day When Princess Almost Became a Caddie

THE OTHER day a chap called doing a survey for a golf magazine. Wanted to know what were my outstanding memories of the last twelve months. He didn't want the obvious ones, like Greg Norman winning the Open or Nick Faldo smiling (and such a nice smile too); he wanted my personal recollections of the season, those times when I strode down the fairway convinced that had I played golf from an early age, they would never have heard of Arnold Palmer.

It was a good time to ask. All I have done of late is stare out of the window watching the wind and rain buffet the bare trees. What I noticed as autumn lengthened into winter was the decreasing amount of foliage in the landscape being matched by a corresponding increase in the amount of clothes worn by the wife as she prepared for a round of golf.

While on the subject, I was recently taken to task by a reader who objects to my use of the term 'the wife'. I am

criticised for being at best patronising, at worst demean-
ing by addressing her in this fashion. All I can say is that
she regularly calls me 'the old man' when in conversation
with others and I have not yet felt the need to write her a
solicitor's letter. What is more, she is called something far
more colourful than 'the wife' when she sinks a fifteen-
foot left-to-right putt to take my money, as she often
does.

Anyway, the wife (for it is she) is nowadays wearing so
much clothing that, combined with her overloaded golf
bag, she becomes a danger to bridges weakened by
structural damage. I envy her determination and fortitude. I am made of softer stuff. I cannot abide golf in cold
and inclement weather. It is not that I am namby-pamby,
rather I suffer from a medical condition known as
Digitus pastinaca, or, to give it a common name, parsnip
fingers. This disability means that whenever it gets cold,
my fingers take on the anaemic colour of parsnips.

I have tried all the remedies. Those sheepskin-lined
mittens seemed the answer, until a friend pointed out I
would play better if I removed them before I hit the ball.
What I really require is a warm golf club. Surely it cannot
be beyond the wit of modern man to invent a set of
centrally heated clubs?

What a revolution that would bring about. Golf in the
Arctic Circle, the Reykjavik Open, a skins in Murmansk,
the next Ryder Cup in Alaska. Instead, what the boffins
have come up with are musical socks. These play your
favourite tune as they are slipped on the feet. It might not
sound much but I believe the invention could have real

significance for the game of golf.

Disciples of the Holloway Musical Golf Swing method (as devised by my friend and golfing partner Lozza Holloway, pianist composer and smooth swinger) will need no explanation of how these socks could be programmed for their benefit. Instead of humming the opening bars of 'The Blue Danube' as we swing we could rely on our socks to do the job for us. It would be an immense load taken from minds already burdened with good advice.

I digress. Back to my golfing year. It started at Gleneagles in May. We were invited to play in the Monarch's Challenge, the tournament officially opening the new Monarch's course designed by Jack Nicklaus. Gleneagles is one of my favourite places on this planet. The Glen is inspiringly beautiful, the hotel sumptuous without being awesome, the courses landscaped by man but with a lot of divine intervention.

We went to bed the night before the practice day in high expectation. It had been a lovely day in mid-May. When we awoke, it was to a perfect winter's morning. There was six inches of snow on the ground and the Ochil Hills looked like they were made of icing sugar.

Jackie Stewart, who was organising the event, sent for supplies of wet-weather gear and thermal underwear. The wet gear arrived safely but the thermal underwear was stuck on Shap Fell where the driver was no doubt much consoled by the load he was carrying. It was not, by any stretch of the imagination, a propitious start.

Overnight, the rain washed most of the snow away

and the big day dawned with the Ochil Hills black with cloud and Mr Nicklaus's baby submerged in flood water.

Our team included Commander Tim Laurence, whose wife, the Princess Royal, decided to come along for the walk. This meant that we were followed by a large gallery including many photographers. Now it is one thing teeing off in front of a crowd, quite another when that crowd trails around with you. Normally, after the first tee, you can forget the spectators and display your incompetence in private, which is how it should be. Not this time.

On the first hole I hit my second shot into a bunker. This greatly intrigued Princess Anne who asked me if there was a particular technique for playing out of sand. I told her what I remembered from the *Gary Player Book of Bunker Play*. When I put it into practice the ball stayed in the trap.

'Mr Parkinson knows what to do but the ball doesn't,' Princess Anne told her husband.

It was an ordinary start and it didn't get any better. Neither my humour nor my reputation was helped by the

fact that my wife was playing ahead of me. Wherever we turned up someone would remind me that Mary had just passed through and had made par net birdie against my double bogey.

'Can I take it Mrs Parkinson is a better golfer than you?' the Princess Royal asked. I was tempted to say that the Queen Mother was probably a better golfer than me on present showing. Instead I nodded miserably. Looking back, I think at that moment I touched the Royal heart and precipitated the extraordinary event that followed.

After we had driven off on the next tee a squall raced down the glen bringing high wind and sleet against our backs. I went to put on my wet gear and discovered that I had left it at the clubhouse. My caddie was sent in a buggy to collect it before the dreaded parsnip syndrome took over my whole body.

I sloshed my way down the fairway to where my drive had landed. With the wind behind I had hit a good shot of 200 yards or more. Looked like a three-wood second shot. It was then I realised I had left my bag on the tee. I squelched all the way back and by the time I returned to my ball there were about three gallons of water in the bag and the woes of the world were on my shoulders. In the meantime my fellow golfers, who had been awaiting my second shot, had played on.

I took my three-wood from the bag and found the grip had all the purchase of a greasy pole. The club spun in my hands and the ball sliced down the fairway into yet another bunker. I was about to curse when I was aware of someone standing behind me. I turned and there was the Princess Royal. She gave me the sort of look you see on the face of animal lovers when they visit Battersea Dogs' Home.

'Would you like me to carry your golf bag?' she asked. Had it been the wife I wouldn't have thought twice.

'You couldn't possibly,' I replied. Now Princess Anne is the wrong person to tell she mustn't do something.

'We'll see about that,' she said and bent to pick up my bag.

At that moment, my caddie came aquaplaning down the fairway in the buggy. Had he not done so I am perfectly convinced I would have walked towards my next shot with a Royal bag-carrier.

Imagine the photograph in the papers, think of what it might have done for my standing at the Royal & Ancient; picture, if you are able, me standing at the clubhouse bar telling the lads, 'As I was saying to my caddie, the Princess Royal, only the other day...'

Contemplate, if you will, the television pictures beamed into every household, and my Auntie Madge in Chesterfield saying, 'Who's that woman carrying our Mike's bag?'

When it comes to who has the best golfing memory of 1993, I rest my case. One further point of interest for royal watchers the world over: if you are ever approached by someone called Tim Laurence for a game of golf and he tells you he has a handicap of 18, play for fun, not money.

February 1994

My Wife Carries Golf Balls in Her Handbag – is She Off Her Trolley?

THE OTHER day, looking for a carrot, I found a golf ball in the vegetable basket. This was not the first time I have discovered golf balls in unlikely places. I have found Titleists in the sock drawer, Pinnacles with the cutlery and Maxflis in the box where we keep our loose

change. I discovered half a dozen balls hiding in an old teapot and once opened the fridge door to find two Slazengers sitting where the eggs ought to be.

I'm thinking of ringing up the Town Hall and asking if they have the golf ball equivalent of the nice woman who came round to get rid of our mice. While she's at it, I'll ask her to exterminate the thousands of golf tees that appear all over our house. The centre of the plague seems to be our bedroom, specifically the wife's make-up table which is covered in golf tees, markers, old scorecards and discarded gloves. When I got married all those years ago this was not what I expected to find in my lady's boudoir.

Apart from all else, golf tees are not ideal bedroom companions. The other day as I was about to pull on a pair of Y-fronts I found a golf tee nestling in the crutch. Imagine the damage that could have caused.

A few years ago in Australia, in an apartment knee-deep in golf tees, the wife woke in the night and on her way to the toilet managed to tread on a tee which speared her foot. The doctor who treated her kept giving me strange looks and it was only when he asked Mary if this sort of thing had happened before I became aware he suspected me of some weird form of wife abuse.

My problem is I live with a woman who doesn't think it strange we share our life with golf equipment. Indeed when I told her I was writing this article she said, 'That reminds me, I must get my old driver out of the wardrobe.' It also reminded me that she keeps golf balls in her handbag. I know this because the other day I asked her if she had any change and in the process of her search she produced half a dozen golf balls from her bag which she placed on the table of the restaurant we were sitting in. The hovering waiter, spotting they were Balatas, said that they were the sort of balls he would play with if could afford them. So we gave them to him instead of a tip.

If my wife carried golf balls about her person as a form of barter then it would make sense. But she doesn't. Why she does remains a mystery, inexplicable, illogical, like woman herself.

My reveries on the strange habits of the person I married were interrupted by terrible news. It was herself on the phone. Her golf trolley had broken down. She was calling on a mobile from the course.

Now you might wonder why a simple matter like a golf trolley packing in should become a crisis. This is because you have never seen my wife's golf bag. It is not so much a receptacle for golf equipment as a way of life.

Mary treats every round of golf as a voyage into the unknown. She has much in common with the early explorers who, believing there was a good chance they would fall off the edge of the world into the fires down below and fearful that every journey might be the last, left nothing to fate and took everything with them.

It is a fair bet in the event of nuclear war breaking out while the wife was in the middle of a round that troops sent in much later to assess the damage would find her living quite happily in a deep bunker on Wentworth golf course. The fact is she is prepared for any eventuality.

In addition to a full complement of golf equipment which includes more balls than you would see lying around on the average practice range, she carries with her a medicine chest equipped for every emergency from headache to snakebite, enough protective clothing to survive a sudden drought or a return to the Ice Age and more food and water than you would require to cross the Gobi Desert on foot.

Hers is the heaviest golf bag I have ever encountered. Caddies flee at her approach. Carrying her bag for eighteen holes is quite beyond the capability of any one man. She would require a line of sherpas. Where other trolleys blithely purr along Mary's contraption groans and wheezes around the course. When it finally packed up on her I knew it had died of overwork.

When she called me to give me the news she did so because she was stranded. There was no question of her carrying the bag back to the clubhouse. It seemed to me that the only way I could rescue her was by hiring a Chinook helicopter. I was spared the expense by the course ranger who mobilised every golf buggy in the immediate vicinity in a rescue operation.

Inspecting the trolley afterwards, the caddie master said it wasn't built to take a load as heavy as my wife's golf bag. When I asked him what was, he suggested an armoured troop carrier such as were used by our lads in the Gulf War.

He doubted if there was a golf trolley on the market with enough power to do the job and said that if one were to be designed to required specifications it would need a specially reinforced frame and a 2.5 litre engine.

While we await a solution, the wife has been forced to

reduce the contents of her golf bag, but she is not happy about it. Nor am I. The excess baggage is all over the house.

Yesterday I found a medicine chest in the cupboard where I keep my priceless collection of jazz LPs, there is a wetsuit in my shirt drawer and golf balls have started appearing for the first time in our bathroom cabinet. I have heard of golf taking over your life but this is ridiculous. Am I living with an obsessive personality or is she trying to tell me something?

If she would stop watching that Nick Faldo golf video I'd ask her.

April 1995

THE MOMENT GARY LINEKER LOST HIS CLAIM TO SAINTHOOD

I HAD this fab idea. Instead of interviewing Gary Lineker face to face why not do the job on the golf course? I could see the headline: A Round With Gary Lineker. But why interview Lineker in the first place? Well, for one thing there is the new career outside football to talk about. How does he think he has done so far? More to the point, are his bosses at the BBC happy?

Also I wanted to talk to him to be reminded that the game of football is still capable of producing men in the tradition of Finney and Charlton; real and proper heroes who proved that being a good sport, a modest man and a well-behaved member of society was not incompatible with becoming a great player and a stern competitor.

In other words I am sick of the ugly side of football, of the in-your-face skinhead, foul-mouthed, yobbish violent aspect of the game. I need the antidote and what better than a round of golf with the man who was never booked in his entire career and who has been called 'The Queen

Mother of football' 'An Evening With Gary Lineker', 'The nicest man on earth' (Spurs fanzine) and 'One of nature's Boy Scouts' (Hunter Davies).

I have to say he cringes at the mention of these descriptions and much prefers the assessment made by Joe Kinnear, the feisty manager of Wimbledon. After Lineker had said that he preferred to watch Teletext than Wimbledon play, Kinnear was asked his opinion of the former captain of England.

'He is,' said Mr Kinnear, 'an arsehole.'

We came together on the first tee of Woburn's Duke's Course, a piece of golfing terrain nearly 7,000 yards long snaking though a forest of trees in glorious countryside near Milton Keynes which has sorted out many a great player.

The first hole is a 514 yard par five. As we surveyed what we had to do, the sun was shining, a light breeze trembled the very tips of the slender pine trees and there were yellow flowers in the gorse. During Lineker's practice swing I positioned myself behind and slightly to his right. It was as if I was fielding at gully. Had I been positioned at old-fashioned deep point I would certainly have been in with a chance of catching his tee-shot which remarkably flew at right angles from his club into the forest.

'Mmmm,' said he, which is not what I would have come out with had I been in his position. During our round I was to marvel at his iron control and limitless patience. It wasn't until much later in the game that he snapped, which is more than can be said for me. After much hacking in the pines, Gary finally hit his ball out of bounds and settled for a blob.

The second hole is a 384 yard par four. Again we were both unconvincing off the tee and I began to see a problem emerging. I am a left-hander with a slice, he is a right-hander with a tendency to hit the ball left to right. That being the case our natural game was designed to take us to different parts of a golf course. Normally this wouldn't matter. However, it is difficult to conduct an interview when both parties are in dense undergrowth on opposite sides of the fairway. When we did finally meet we were sharing a bunker.

'We're crazy. We came on the course without warming up and expect to play well. It's silly,' said Lineker. I didn't tell him that I hated practice and that my idea of warming up was a double egg, sausage, bacon and fried bread breakfast which I had managed to scoff that morning. I did the decent thing and sympathised.

I told him that when I once complained about playing badly, the golf pro I was with said, 'It's your own fault. You walk on to a course without preparing yourself. You never see a pro do that.' I said something sarcastic like that was because pros had nothing else to do. He said, 'Let me ask you a question. When you do a show on television do you rehearse?' I said we did. 'That's exactly what we do,' he said.

Lineker managed a wan smile at my homespun wisdom. At the time he was knee-deep in sand looking at an impossible shot on to a sloping green and thinking he would settle for a double bogey. Could it be I am losing my sense of timing?

The third hole on the Duke's course is one of the most photogenic in British golf. It is a 134 yard par three across a valley to a green far below. The hole is surrounded by trees and rhododendrons. It was here that Gary Lineker showed his mettle. He hit a high, soft nine-iron to within fifteen feet but left the ball above the pin. When the sun shines and the greens are running this is a bit like putting down a glacier. He nicked the cup with his first putt and holed from six feet coming back for a par.

We can now talk golf. He played first as a teenager but gave it up when he became a professional footballer. He started playing again when he went to Japan. He hasn't got a handicap but thinks 20 or 22 might be fair at present and hopes to get down to single figures. No reason why he shouldn't. He's got a slow, rhythmic swing, a calm temperament and a self-belief that comes with being a top-class professional athlete.

When we recommenced our round we played quietly and without much incident until the eighth hole when there was a most remarkable occurrence. Lineker hit his drive into the trees. He called that he had located his ball and the next sound I heard was a ball hitting timber followed by quiet. More scuffling in the undergrowth and then terrible clatter as a ball seemed to strike four or five trees before silence descended once more.

As I waited on the fairway, my ears as sensitive as tuning forks to any indication of what might be happening to my opponent, there came the crack of ball on tree followed this time by an anguished cry of 'Shit!' It is the moment Gary Lineker lost his claim to sainthood. It was so unexpected I'm thinking of sponsoring a commemorative plaque on a tree at the spot where it happened.

I only mention the incident because it does Gary Lineker a disservice to portray him as a sickeningly perfect goody-goody with a halo and whipped cream for blood. Any athlete who gets to the top has to be tough, mentally and physically. Lineker's self-control and patience are part of his physical toughness just as his ability to learn quickly using a mind which is not befuddled by either booze or fame is an indication of his mental strength.

Auntie is very much taken with Gary Lineker, and the feeling is mutual. Lineker is heading off down the media super highway on yet another episode in an extraordinary career. Will it end there? Will being a witness to events be as fulfilling as becoming a shaper of the future? He would love to help decide the direction his sport takes in years to come and thinks it sad that soccer tends to ignore its great names.

As we approached the final hole on a day when we had been soundly beaten by the course, he said, 'Sometimes I hate this game and sometimes I love it. Today I think I hate it.' Then he knocked in a fifteen-footer for a par and changed his mind.

As I walked off the course a man who must have thought I was Lineker's minder or, alternatively, possessed a kindly face, asked me if I could get him the star's autograph. I said he should make a direct approach as

Lineker was not renowned for assaulting autograph hunters.

'Where's he off to?' the man said.

'He's going up to Leicester,' I answered.

'Why?' the man asked.

'He's going to be given the Freedom of the City in order that he might graze his sheep near the town hall,' I said.

'Quite right, too,' said the man as if it was the only sensible thing to be done for the likes of Gary Lineker; which it is.

April 1995

No Escape for Player with the Secret Touch

IT DIDN'T take me long to get a free golf lesson from Gary Player. What he said was, 'How are you?' An innocent enough question but it cost him dear. I said, 'I'm all right except for this crick in my neck caused by a faulty golf swing.' I could see the panic in his eyes but there was no escape.

'I was wondering,' I said, 'if you might have a look and see what I am doing wrong.' Gary swallowed a handful of vitamin pills. He had seen me play and knew he needed to be strong to face what was ahead.

His predicament is a common one for golf professionals. Theirs is the only job I can think of where the practitioners are expected to pass on their secrets.

I was once at a party with Ian Baker-Finch when he was asked by the hostess to show her how to play out of bunkers. From that point on the entire *soirée* took place in sand with canapes and drinks being served as Mr Baker-Finch – immaculate in evening dress – gave lessons to the assembly.

The point is that the hostess wouldn't dream of asking

Pete Sampras for a quick lesson on the backhand cross-court volley, nor would her husband have required Mike Atherton to demonstrate the cover drive or Shane Warne to reveal the secrets of his googly.

When I interviewed Pavarotti I didn't ask him to teach me how to sing 'Nessun Dorma', and when interviewing Sir Alec Guinness it never crossed my mind to request a quick lesson in acting. He did slightly pre-empt the situation by telling me that whenever he was asked the secret of acting he would always say, 'Remember, before you go on stage, to cough and check your flies.'

So what did Gary tell me? He said cricked necks and back pains in golfers of my age were nature's way of telling us we required a change of method. Super Seniors like yourself (people aged sixty and above) should narrow and slightly close the stance at address and use a much stronger grip on the club. I have decided to change from the Vardon overlap to the ten-fingers, two-fisted method. This, according to my coach, gives a better hand action through the ball and therefore more power.

However, the most important change is to learn how to 'walk through' the ball. This means transferring your weight at impact and continuing to walk after the ball. Mr Player reckons that if you follow this procedure, back strains disappear and you may once again become a force to be reckoned with in the mid-week swindle. He sent me on my way with a signed copy of his book *Golf Begins At 50* and the inscription 'Play Well'.

Easier said than done. My problem is walking after the ball. What I find is if I hit the ball, I don't walk through.

Then if I concentrate on walking rather than hitting, I walk with great style but leave the ball on the peg. I tested my new technique in the red-hot furnace of the Wentworth married couples foursomes.

It had been a while since I played with the wife. Indeed it had been a while since I had seen her at all. The reason for our estrangement was her involvement with the Wentworth ladies' golf team who have just won the Pearson Trophy, a prestigious interclub and county championship.

This triumph was not achieved without sacrifice, mainly by the husbands who were left at home while their wives rampaged through Surrey and environs in search of trophies. Even when our wives reappeared in the family home they were not the same.

It is the little things you pick up on when you have been married for a while. For instance, I was giving the wife a welcoming cuddle one morning when I realised she was smelling of fish. We are not the sort of people who eat kippers early in the day. She caught me wrinkling my nose.

'Smoked salmon,' she explained.

'For breakfast?' I asked.

'And every other meal,' she said. She told me the team had been put on a smoked salmon diet as part of their training schedule. For a month she ate nothing but smoked salmon and bananas. Once, going through her golf bag to find some keys, I came across two forgotten bananas, black and shrivelled like the dried fruit we used to buy during the war.

The ladies of Wentworth left nothing to chance. Field Marshal Montgomery could not have planned a more detailed campaign. Indeed, the kitchen of my house came to resemble the operational centre of an army on the move. Golf courses were targeted and analysed, hole by hole; swing thoughts were stuck to the refrigerator; aerial photographs were commissioned.

Every table in our house was so covered in maps that for a month I ate from a tray on my knees. Detailed plans were drawn up of journeys from Wentworth to Woking and the like. Dummy runs were operated with the team arriving triumphantly in the opposition's car park and celebrating their map-reading triumph with high fives before driving off again leaving the locals wondering what the heck was going on.

Even so there were disasters. My wife, who needs a road map to get to the bottom of our street, became confused on one journey and stopped a bus to ask the way. The driver, no doubt in a state of shock at having been waved down by a mad woman carrying a three-iron, proved unhelpful so the wife boarded the bus only to find it full of Japanese tourists on their way to Wisley to see the botanical gardens.

The neglected victims of this madness – the husbands who became baffled onlookers at their wives' sporting ambitions – took to 'phoning one another for reassurance. One man told me that his wife spent so much time at the golf club he had to take her pet spaniel to work with him.

'I have spent so much time with the dog I can now speak Cocker,' he said, proudly.

What I am thinking of doing is cocooning our kitchen and leaving it as it is, maps and all, rather like Winston Churchill's bunker in Whitehall. For a small charge, visitors might see how a women's golf team conquered the world.

Therefore the married couples foursomes competition at Wentworth was more than a game of golf; it was a reunion and a chance to test my new swing designed by Gary Player.

I wish I could report that Mary and I celebrated our reunion with a victory. We played badly and scored only 25 points. My excuse is that the new swing needs a bit more work. Mary reckons her loss of form was due to a sense of anti-climax after winning a Major. In other words, playing with me no longer has the magic it once had. I don't think she fancies the idea of being seen with a Super Senior.

I wonder how she will cope with her new-found fame as a golfer. What will she do the first time someone asks her for advice? I would tell them to buy a smoked salmon sandwich and a road map and be done with it.

August 1995

Putting Nightmare Leaves Augusta's Greens in the Shade

ONE DAY I will go to Augusta and check out those greens for myself. What I suspect is that while putting might be difficult, the problem is nothing compared to holing out on hollow tined greens in April with the rain dripping down your neck and the putter grip like a bar of soap, that is if you can feel it, which you can't because your hands fell off from frostbite two holes before.

I don't buy all those horror stories about starting a putt in Georgia and it finishing in Alabama. Chance would be a fine thing. The most famous image of the greens at Augusta is the one requiring us to imagine putting the ball from the roof of a car and getting it to stop on the bonnet. It doesn't impress me. Far more difficult is starting the ball on the bonnet, knocking it up the windscreen and stopping it on the roof while using a polo mallet, which is what it is like putting on British courses at present.

Putting Nightmare

Compared to the average club golfer, the pros are a pampered lot. They've forgotten what it's like to play on ploughed fairways where a blade of grass is likely to be the subject of a preservation order. They don't know what it's like to lose your ball under a mountain of rotting leaves or find a half-eaten jackdaw on the putting surface. When we find our ball in an unplayable lie, there is no friendly official on hand to give us relief on the grounds that it has come to rest on a pile of weasel droppings.

Similarly, when we overdrive the green there are no spectators to prevent the ball going out of bounds. In other words, if Sam Torrance and Seve Ballesteros thought they had a bad time at Augusta, let me tell them it was nothing compared to what I suffered at Temple Golf Club the other day.

Competing in the midweek medal, I shot a gross 93, net 80, and played like a pillock. I blame the greens. It was like putting on a surface of soggy toast. On one occasion my ball reached the lip and then hopped in the air and over the hole like a man jumping a puddle. What is more, I was distracted by one of my playing partners, Mr Lynch, who was wearing what appeared to be a tea-cosy on his head and what looked like a pair of diving boots on the opposite end.

The third member of our team, Mr Holloway, the piano player, had a committee meeting to go to and played the round *con brio* instead of his usual *larghetto*. What is more, I had a bad back and the battery on my trolley packed up coming up the hill on the seventeenth.

You can tell I had a good time. If you are an experienced golfer, you will also realise I am doing what all of us do after a lousy round, namely covering up my deficiencies with excuses.

I had started in optimistic mood. Having come from practice in Australia, where I played quite well, I imagined I would continue the form and have an advantage over my companions who had been denied golf in frozen Britain. In fact the opposite happened.

They performed as if they had never been off a golf course and I played as if I'd never been on one. It was a triumph for hibernation over migration. There are some people who actually look forward to winter golf. They welcome the excuse to play in the cold and wet because it gives them a legitimate reason for a large drink before and sometimes during the round. And the fact they play better sozzled than I do sober is yet further proof of the efficacy of drugs in sport.

Putting Nightmare

Anyone who knows me at all will be aware I am not averse to a drink. But never on a golf course. Fact is, even after one I lose whatever timing and rhythm I might possess. Lord knows I have tried. I once played with the late, lamented Peter Cooke in Spain when he arrived on the tee with a caddie carrying two golf bags, one for the clubs and the other for the booze. Peter, a generous man, invited me to partake of his mobile cocktail cabinet.

He also offered a heart-starter to the caddie, who took a bottle of vodka by the neck and drank it like lemonade. On the seventh hole, the caddie fell asleep with his head on the bags and we kept him company under a tree until a passing greenkeeper returned us to the clubhouse in his truck.

We learnt from the experience. It cured me of drink and Peter of caddies.

So if winter golf is unacceptable, what takes its place? I may have stumbled across the alternative. I was invited to play a game in Studio One at the BBC Television Centre, where Jimmy Tarbuck was hosting a new show based on golf. The game was played on a three-dimensional golf simulator with a screen large enough to give the impression you really were standing on the tee and looking down the fairway. You struck the ball in front of three sensors which tracked the path of its flight and the information was flashed on screen. It was a sophisticated version of a computer game and might have a more important use for the more serious player than a game show where the golfer was teamed with a member of the public who assisted by answering questions for yards.

For instance, when I drove off and the computer told me I had hit the ball 200 yards, leaving 300 yards to the pin, my partner advanced me down the fairway by answering questions worth distance instead of points. Because she could name the first man on the moon, and knew the difference between a cosmonaut and an astronaut, not only did she win a trip to California but she also reduced a monster par five on a championship course in Utah to two three-woods and a putt. Easy.

The R & A must look at this innovation. I have no doubt that Sky Television already have and can foresee a time in future Ryder Cups when players' wives and girlfriends sit in the National Lottery studio and are asked questions by Anthea Turner. Can you imagine the fate of the Ryder Cup depending on Bernhard Langer's wife knowing if rhubarb is a fruit or a vegetable? You may snigger, but it could happen. In fact it already has. My opponent at the TV Centre was my wife. The last time I beat her at golf Arnold Palmer was a lad, but I won the money (for charity) not because I played better but because her partner didn't know about rhubarb and mine did.

Since my golfing fortunes changed for the better, my marriage has taken a turn for the worse. It is not that my wife is a bad loser, she has simply forgotten what it is like not to win.

Our situation was exacerbated over the weekend because I had backed Greg Norman for the Masters and her money was on Nick Faldo. She suspects me of being a closet Australian. For all the splendour of the golf in

Putting Nightmare

Augusta, I couldn't help thinking how much more difficult the game would be if an approach shot depended upon the players knowing the name of the first dog in space, or how to spell Mississippi.

Until they have played Studio One of the TV Centre, they don't know the meaning of pressure. Like I said, pampered.

April 1996

Discovering the Meaning of Life – and Only my Wife was There as a Witness

I CAN'T keep it to myself any longer. I have had my first hole-in-one. It happened three weeks ago, on a desert course in Arizona witnessed only by my wife and a pair of circling hawks, so you will have to take my word for it. It was a 120 yard par three carved into the base of Camelback Mountain near Scottsdale.

Behind me and to one side there were cacti, scorpions and rattlesnakes (I love a drama), leading to the kind of ridge John Ford used to cram with Apache whenever John Wayne was in trouble.

High on the tee, I looked down to the green, where the pin was placed rear left. There was a slight wind, no more than a zephyr, in my face as I drew my trusty pitching wedge from the bag. I had been playing so badly my only ambition was to keep the ball in Arizona. As it was, it sang off the club, the ball tracing an arc against the blue desert sky (riveting isn't it?). When it pitched it bounced twice and then rolled slowly into the hole.

'Did you see what I saw?' I asked the wife. She was dumbstruck, and could only nod. It is difficult to describe my emotions at that moment.

First of all I wished I had been playing with my regular golfing partners, Messrs Barratt and Holloway. Together we have stoically endured the despair golf can cause and we deserve the odd moment of glory. I also wished the spectator who laughed at my swing in a pro-am at Stoke Poges in 1983 had been on hand to say he was sorry.

It would have been nice if the TV cameras had been present so I could have told Steve Rider my achievement was the result of years of practice and not to mention my trust in the Big Golf Coach in the Sky, not to mention my agent, Mr McCormack, my family, whom I neglected in my search for the perfect swing, and my Uncle Jim who

gave me my first golf club when I was forty-seven (I am something of a late developer).

What is more, any manufacturer looking for a mature version of Tiger Woods to sponsor will need to know that I was dressed almost entirely by Messrs Marks and Spencer except for Calvin Klein underpants and my shoes, which are so old they would only interest a Museum of National Costume.

On the other hand, I have no real wish to capitalise upon my achievement. I don't want it to change my life in any way.

A hole-in-one is as much a rite of passage as hearing your first four-letter-word at a football match; singing Eskimo Nell on your first rugby tour; or finding out the meaning of life when hit on the box from a quick bowler. The emotions are too deep and personal to be shared.

I have divulged my secrets because you might have detected a certain insouciance in my manner which was lacking before. This is entirely due to the fact I have just joined a very exclusive club. And you haven't.

It must be said golf in America is not like playing at home. It is much better. You notice the difference upon arrival when the car is parked for you. Your clubs are taken away and the next time you see them is on the buggy or awaiting you on the first tee. After the game the clubs are cleaned and placed back in the car.

In the pro shop the staff are both plentiful and eager to help. As you part with your money you believe they want you to have a good time. It is a strictly commercial transaction but at least in America the service industry is geared to promoting the feeling you are getting value for money. Can we say the same here?

I wonder what Americans think when they visit a British golf course where, generally speaking, what they take for granted at their own club is not even a remote possibility. I played about a dozen courses during my visit and on every occasion was able to practise on an immaculate practice range at no extra cost and using proper golf balls. Contrast this to the situation here where, in the unlikely event of there being a practice facility, it is odds-on you will play off mats and almost certain that the balls will be those yellow granite jobs which spew out of an antiquated machine after the insertion of a token purchased from the pro who ought to be ashamed of himself.

Similarly, after paying for a day's golf they might feel entitled to get the hump when asked to cough up for tees and markers, something which never happened to me in America. Nor did I pay for a course guide. Moreover, what about finishing the round only to find the bar has closed or else the chef went home at 3 p.m. In America it is written into the constitution that people eat as much as they can any time they feel like it.

There are chuck wagons on the course just in case you fancy a bite between shots and on three or four of the courses we played, at the approach to the halfway house we were able to phone ahead and order the refreshment of our choice. When we can put men into space, we shouldn't wonder at such things. The Americans don't. We do.

We invented the game but have not understood the need to move on. Golf like cricket and one or two other institutions in Britain not to do with sport, is stultified by tradition.

Nonetheless it was good to be back. To stand on the first tee at Temple and look across the valley to Marlow and beyond is enough to make the dictum that golf is a good walk spoiled seem more churlish than witty. A mere game cannot compare with a view like that. I was re-united with my partner Lozza Holloway, whose game is based upon notes he writes to himself and places in a holder atop his golf bag.

'Ben Hogan' is a reminder of the great man's instruction that at address the golfer should imagine himself standing with his head through a pane of glass which at no time during the swing should be touched by the club. 'Johann Strauss' on the other hand tells Lozza to regulate his swing to the opening notes of 'The Blue Danube'.

I favoured 'Ta, ra, ra, boom, dee, ay' for a while but to no avail. At present, for reasons about to be made clear, I am experimenting with certain parts of the 'Messiah' in the hope I might break 90 regularly if I get the Good Lord interested. The link between golf and music is not a new idea but it has been given an added dimension in an article I read in an American golf magazine.

The author, a Dr Tomasi, argues that practising golf to a full orchestral work will not only give you the right rhythm with which to swing the club but will, if chosen carefully, relax the mind and body to that state of nirvana known in common sporting parlance as 'the zone'.

He suggests Vivaldi, Handel or Bach as being best suited to the job. He also says the way to a grooved swing is to practise to a favourite pop song so that when you hum it on the course it will trigger the appropriate response. Dr Tomasi makes the point this music has to be chosen with particular care. For instance, it is no use choosing a song which is a favourite because of, let us say, a romantic association. It would be no good at all humming 'As Time Goes By' for a swing trigger if all it does is conjure up memories of a barmaid at Butlin's in Clacton many years ago.

As things turned out, Johann Strauss had it over George Frederic Handel. In other words Lozza's swing was more musical than mine though neither could be described as a thing of beauty. So much for the 'Hallelujah Chorus'. Next time I'll try something quieter. 'Comfort Ye' seems just about right for both tempo and sentiment.

April 1977

In the Swing at the Cradle of Golf

STAND back while I wax lyrical. From the raised tee, I could see the sunlight sparkling on the lightly ruffled waters of the sea. White clouds peeked over the tops of the distant mountains. Through the woods, I glimpsed Skibo Castle and over the loch, near the salmon ladder, an osprey circled.

It was a moment to embrace nature, to forget that only a short distance from where I was standing, ships from Iceland were chugging along, carrying their loads of used fivers to the well-known ports of Nottingham and White Hart Lane, vessels of the well-known Hauge Line with names like *SS Venabung* or *SS Bungclough*.

But cease. I am becoming intoxicated with the sweet Highland air, which is like wine. We are playing the Carnegie Links, designed by Donald Steel, a course as lovely as it is testing. Golf was first played here a hundred years ago when Andrew Carnegie, who lived in Skibo Castle when he wasn't making billions in America, took up the game. He wasn't very good but hated losing and guests were told they had a better chance of being invited back if the host won.

I would have been the perfect guest. In my present form, I would finish last in a match against Lord Nelson, Long John Silver and Little Nell. Peter de Savary bought the castle, put Donald Steel to work on the golf course and founded the Carnegie Club, creating the ambience of a great Edwardian sporting estate where the members are treated as house guests. With my regular partner, the estimable and formidable Mary Parkinson, I played three rounds at Carnegie without ever threatening the course record. On the other hand, every step was an exploration of golf's genius for making a good walk an unforgettable experience.

This part of the world is where golf started. Royal Dornoch, where golf has been played since 1616, is only four miles away. The perceptive American golf writer Herbert Warren Wind described Royal Dornoch as 'the most natural course in the world', and said that no golfer worth his salt had completed his education until he had played and studied the course.

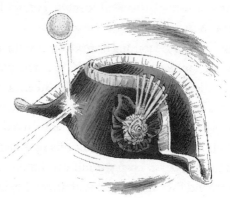

'It conveys to the modern golfer the evocation of golf at its best,' he wrote. And so it does, except he must have played the course before it was used by the RAF as an area where their planes practise strafing and bombing. The noise and pollution created by these awful machines would be intolerable anywhere but it is particularly sad than an area of such noble beauty should be so mal-treated.

I am only a simple golfer so maybe they'll forgive me if I ask who they are practising invading? Couldn't they play their games out to sea? Why don't they use simu-lators? Or is it just a case of boys with toys? In any event, all I took away with me from Royal Dornoch was a headache because of the incessant noise and a feeling of great sympathy for the locals who have to suffer the curse.

Otherwise, the trip to the cradle of golf was blissful. There was one day when the wind was such you could lean against it. 'A five-club wind,' said the caddie. Mary said she felt unwell because she had 'eaten too much wind'. What a marvellous title for a book: *Eating Wind. A Beginner's Guide To Links Golf.*

The rest of the time, it was warm enough for shorts. Not that I wore them. I cannot abide those long socks. In America, I play in shorts all the time because they generally don't insist upon knee length hose. Most of the courses I play in Australia follow the British example and require long socks. Had the French settled Australia, things might have been very different. For one thing we would have stood a better chance of beating them at cricket. Captain Cook has a lot to answer for. What I want to know is why women can play in short socks but men cannot and while we are about it, why are members' dogs allowed bare-legged on most golf courses? I am thinking of taking my case to the European Court of Appeal.

But back to where we started this reverie, standing on the tee of the seventeenth hole at Carnegie Links studying the problem it posed: a short par four, only 290 yards to the centre of the green but across a moat of deep bunkers and into a strong cross wind from the sea. The course guide says: 'Almost reachable in some conditions. The player who tries must flirt with the sea and swing the ball left to right in the wind.'

That's one way of playing it. On the other hand, you could follow my example, which involved mishitting a drive to the rim of a fairway bunker, hacking an eight-iron to within hailing distance of the flag and then thinning a chip, which skittered across the green, collided with the flag pole and plopped into the hole. At the clubhouse, the pro asked how we had done.

'Made a three at the seventeenth,' I said.

'Not many do that,' he said.

'Not like I did, they don't,' I said. Whistling 'My Way' I retired to my castle for the night. There is nothing so smug or self-satisfied as a lucky golfer.

September 1997

Play Slows to Crawl as Manual Mania Brings Golfers to Their Knees

D R SANDY MATHEWSON is my hero. Already he has my nomination for Sports Personality of the Year, 1998. As captain of the Royal and Ancient he has embarked upon a crusade to rid golf of the curse of slow play.

Dr Mathewson says no player should take more than three and a half hours for a round. He blamed the example set by some professionals but suggested another reason at club level was that the proper way to play was not being passed from generation to generation. He suggests clubs conduct etiquette tests to ensure golfers are fit to be allowed on the course. These are matters of the utmost importance.

There is nothing guaranteed to bring out the vile nature of man more than being trapped behind a slow fourball. Anyone who has been in that situation and

never contemplated murder of his fellow man, or geno-
cide if the culprits happen to be foreign, or something
worse if they are women, has a strong chance of becoming a saint in Mr Blair's next Honours List.

The etiquette of golf demands that you wait patiently
until called through. If the invitation is tardy, a member
of your team must walk ahead and politely suggest it
might be a good idea if they stood aside in the interests of
keeping the course moving. The messenger must resist
any temptation to embellish the request with observations such as it would be nice to complete the round
before lighting up time, or on the same day as we set off,
or before the completion of the Millennium Dome. Indeed if his suggestion is refused there is nothing he can do
about it but wait until the round is finished and have a
quiet word in the bar or complain to the secretary in the
hope he will have them publicly flogged on the putting
green before the next monthly Stableford.

It would be reassuring to believe, as Dr Mathewson
does, that etiquette tests will do the trick and remind
golfers the game is much better played briskly and with
good manners. In this technological age it is much more
likely that modern science will prove the best way of
improving matters. It is rumoured plans are already
advanced for a system whereby teams are given a smart
card with which they clock in at the first tee and at
regular intervals throughout the round. Thus an accurate
check is made on their progress and a precise time kept
on the round. If they take more than the three and a half
hours suggested by the captain of the Royal and Ancient

their scores will be adjusted accordingly. A one-shot penalty is proposed for every five minutes over the limit. Thus someone who has played to level par and fancies his chances for the Captain's Prize but has taken thirty minutes longer than he ought will finish six over. Seems fair enough to me.

Persistent offenders will be given yellow cards and three of these mean automatic suspension for two weeks, during which time the culprits will be required for latrine duty. In the case of foreigners, particularly Japanese and Germans, there is a Home Office document being drawn up looking into the possibility of having them deported. If the offenders are women, they will be sent on rehabilitation courses to reacquaint them with the traditional virtues of ironing, step-scrubbing and black-leading the fireplace.

It would also help if there weren't so many instruction books about how to play golf. There are more golf books than sex manuals, surely the clearest indication yet that we have our priorities in the wrong order. Why only the other day Mrs Parkinson informed me that all my problems would be solved if I put more stomach into it. She had, I must inform you, been reading *How to Play Better Golf* rather than *How to Get the Best Out of Your Old Man*. When I asked her to explain this mysterious observation she said, 'Hit it with your stomach.'

I don't know exactly what it means. All I do know is it will be added to the ever lengthening litany modern golfers are brainwashed into trying to remember before they ever put club to ball. As they stand on the tee they must remind themselves they are perched on the edge of a bar stool with their necks through an imaginary pane of glass gripping the club with sufficient pressure to strangle a healthy gerbil.

Next they have to remember to take the club back slowly until reaching a position where the club is horizontal with the ground, the back is toward the hole, the head is over the ball and the right elbow is not flapping. What now? Pulling the club down as if ringing a church bell and transferring weight through the ball, the golfer must remember to accelerate his hands through the point of impact and finish high. Providing he has remembered all this advice, plus the latest intelligence about hitting the ball with the stomach, the golfer stands a fair chance of striking the pill, always providing he remembered that other pearl of wisdom: tee it high, watch it fly.

When you add this to two practice swings, a course chart, an argument about how to convert metres into yards, much messing about with grass and portable wind socks followed by close scrutiny of surrounding woodland to assess the likelihood of the swing being interrupted by rutting deer, you begin to see how the years can pass by without much to show.

There are only two pieces of advice every golfer should understand and follow. The first is Arnold Palmer's dictum on how to play the game: 'Hit it hard, go find it and hit it hard again', while at the same time bearing in mind the injunction: 'By the time you get to your ball if you don't know what to do with it, try another sport.'

January 1998

The Pain of Jake's Progress Proves that Four's a Crowd

THE golf course at the Phoenician Hotel hugs Camel-back Mountain where cacti stand like sentinels on the rim and the desert blooms in pink and yellow flowers. If I wax lyrical it is only because I share the course with hummingbirds and hawks, jack rabbits and lizards. At one hole, where you park your buggy and climb the steps to a tee cut into the mountain, a gang of chipmunks under contract to Disney observes your departure before invading the vehicle looking for food. There are signs warning of rattlesnakes which, I fancy, are more a talking point for tourists than a public safety announcement. Nonetheless, my imitation of a rattlesnake delivered as my wife reaches the top of her backswing is the most effective way I have yet devised of beating Mary.

The only problem we have is that of being a twoball in a fourball society. Holiday golf is designed for four players which means a twosome like us being paired with strangers on the first tee. It is like an arranged marriage: sometimes it works, more often than not it is a complete disaster. Jake from New Jersey said he was a 24 handicapper. It proved to be a generous assessment of his ability to hit a golf ball. He was equipped with the latest technology, carbon shafts, titanium balls, plutonium woods. He would have been better served by a croquet mallet. He insisted on playing from the championship tees and was only dissuaded from fulfilling his foolish ambition after nine interminable holes by the intervention of the course marshall, who pointed out we were holding up play so badly the golfers behind us were building shelters for the night and the management had set up soup kitchens and group counselling.

Top of Jake's problems as a golfer was his inability to hit the ball further than fifty yards no matter which club he chose. This was entirely due to his habit of playing the ball so far outside his left foot even a straight-faced club sliced under the ball created a high, spinning lob. After every shot, he would curse and pose the rhetorical question, 'What am I doing wrong?'

Answer came there none. We know a hopeless cause when we see one. Like all slob golfers, Jake possessed neither the sense nor the manners to give up when his situation became hopeless. He was undoubtedly the most awful putter I have ever seen. He was awesomely bad. I do not exaggerate when I say his judgment of line and length were such that a blindfold would only have improved matters.

On average, he took five putts to get within the shadow of the flag. He was a serial putter, the kind who pursues the ball to the hole with total disregard for putting in turn or trampling an opponent's lines.

Like all players who do not understand the conviviality of the game, he had no concept of sharing a round with his partners. Only once did he remark on an opponent's shot. He was standing next to me as I played my second shot across a lake to the green on the last hole.

By this time, I was past caring. It was 210 yards to the pin and I hit a five-wood which landed on the water ten feet from shore, hippety-hopped on the surface and skipped on to the green to finish four feet from the pin.

'Jeez. What happened?' said Jake.

'Did you not see the gloved hand of the Lady of the Lake catch the ball and lob it on to the green?' I asked. He was unimpressed.

'You couldn't do that again if you played golf until you were a hundred,' he said.

What I wanted to say was that if ever I did repeat the

shot, the only certainty was he wouldn't be in the same fourball. But I didn't. Instead, I smiled at a flowering cactus and waved at a passing hummingbird. Who wants ructions in paradise?

April 1998

CAPTAIN'S DAY
HORRORS

Rough Justice on the Back Nine of Life

I HAVE never been one for early morning golf. Mid-morning tee-off is quite soon enough for me, mainly because my limbs don't start receiving messages from my brain until about 10 a.m. I made an exception at the weekend because one of my partners, Lozza Holloway, the piano player, had a gig later in the day and the third member of the team, the journalist and broadcaster Michael Barratt, simply likes playing early, mainly I suspect, because of the years he spent as a knocker-upper in his native Leeds.

Also it was Captain's Day, a chance to achieve golfing immortality by getting our names on the clubhouse wall. Most of all it was an opportunity to play the course when it had been pampered and cossetted for a special day. Unlike the rest of us, it looked a picture. Even under slate grey skies, the view from the high first tee across the valley to Bisham and Marlow justified the membership fees.

On a still day, the opening hole at Temple Golf Club is as hospitable as it is beautiful. However, when the wind whistles up the fairway and flattens your trouser legs against the horizon, then it is not the hole at which you want to commence a medal round. Lozza Holloway, who is the steadiest and best golfer of the three, teed off at 6.50 for the first time, 6.55 for a second time and at 7 for the third and final time. There was, he thought, a touch of wind-induced Scarlatti in his swing. Whatever the reason, it did not augur well. The last time he lost two golf balls he was playing in Geraldo's band.

He took a nine on the first hole, I made a six. My drive would have gone further had it been hit by Lena Zavaroni, my seven-iron from the rough nearly broke my wrists, my approach ended in a grass bunker to the right of the green whereupon I chipped to within three feet of the hole. I would have been satisfied with a bogey five. However, my putt was of the palsied variety and I knew then that this was but the overture to a full-scale horror.

To be frank with you, I was not in the right frame of mind. I had prepared well. I had gone to bed early the night before with nothing more damaging than a cup of herbal tea. I had read *Power Driving, The Key To Distance and Accuracy*, pondered *The Art of the Short Game* and devoured *Putting Made Simple*. My game-plan was to keep the driver in the bag until the back nine and concentrate on keeping the ball on the fairway. My thought for the day was swing slow, finish high. I was programmed for success.

What sabotaged my plan was a question our secretary asked when we signed on at the clubhouse. He said to me 'I take it you will be entering the veterans' competition.' I suddenly realised I had qualified without being aware of my new status. The trick of growing older is to ignore the passing years. The problem is that other people won't let you. The last time I was confronted with the fact that I am no longer the lissom youth I see in my mind's eye was when an air hostess answered my complaint about bad service by patting me on the head and saying, 'There, there, old man. Keep your hair on.'

What is particularly saddening about my arrival on the back nine of life, so to speak, is that as far as golf is concerned, I didn't spend too much time on the front nine. It wasn't until my mid forties that I relinquished my job as chairman and founder member of the Anti-Golf Society and started playing the game. I have gone very quickly from rabbit to veteran without acquiring a real history. It is as if I was born at the age of forty-five. Looking back to Saturday's game, I can see it was this confrontation with my own mortality prompted by our secretary's innocent question that upset my delicately balanced bio-rhythms.

If this sounds a trifle high falutin' you ain't heard nothing yet. I believe that there is a mystical element in golf which often is the difference between a successful round and selling your clubs. Señor Ballesteros is the most eminent example of my theory. He has started winning again, looking again like the greatest golfer in the world.

Not too long ago some were writing him off. What has happened? Well the experts say he has changed his putter. They seek a practical solution and by doing so make my point. Is it a magic putter? Does it bear special qualities? Should we rush out and buy one and expect our game to improve?

Of course not. The fact is no one, not even Seve, knows what is happening. You dare not ask in case it goes away, whatever it might be. It happens to all of us from time to time. We play a round of golf and suddenly it seems the easiest game in the world. The ball sings from the club, the chips roll to the pin, the putts drop. Other times you play like a dead donkey. Why? Who can tell. What we do know is that there never was a worried man who played a decent round of golf; which is how I explain my awful performance on Captain's Day.

It is to my credit that it took a while for the wheels to come off. I struck the ball quite well but I couldn't putt. I tried the Crenshaw upright technique as well as the crouched style with the putter at 45 degrees to the green as favoured by Tommy Nakajima. None of it worked. I was thinking of trying Herr Langer's method. That's how golf can drive you crazy.

The rot really set in on the seventh, a benign par four. Michael Barratt, who had been playing solidly, struck his second shot into the greenside bunker. There is nothing more risible in all of sport than a golfer dressed and equipped like Nick Faldo trying to play a ball out of sand; which is why golf is the ultimate test of sportsmanship and manners.

Bunkers have destroyed golfers, turned strong men into gibbering wrecks. They are the ultimate obstacles in life, the supreme test of character. I have played with men who have thrown all their clubs, followed by their bag and the trolley over cliffs after spending too long in a bunker. Sometimes they had to be restrained from following their equipment onto the rocks below. I have also played with men who, faced with similar disasters, were so incredibly brave and humorous it made you proud to be marking their card. One chap I played with took six shots to get out of the bunker at Gleneagles and then putted back into the same bunker. All he said was, 'What a nuisance.'

Therefore, when Michael Barratt stood in the bunker, sand-iron poised, he felt nothing but sympathy and best wishes flowing towards him from Lozza Holloway and myself. He was sitting in the middle of the bunker on flat sand so we didn't anticipate too much drama. His first shot lifted the ball in the air, which is the general idea, but didn't move it forward so it plopped back to something like its original position.

'Oh dear,' said Michael.

'Hard luck,' we said. His second shot did exactly the same.

'Damn,' said Michael. We made reassuring sounds. His third shot moved the ball forward but not up in the air. He was doing all the right things but not at the same time. 'What is going on?' he asked. It was a rhetorical question. At the fourth attempt, he drove the ball into the face of the bunker. The crisis was increasing all the time, as were the comic possibilities.

'How many have I had in the bunker?' asked Michael. 'Four,' we told him. He looked so forlorn we wanted to adopt him. His next shot hit the underside lip of the bunker and flew behind him.

'What am I doing wrong?' he asked. Lozza suggested he take more sand. I managed to refrain from observing that there wasn't much left in the bunker, most of it having been deposited on the green which looked like Clacton beach.

Attempting to follow instructions and by now a desperate man, Michael took a lot of sand but no ball in his next attempt. As a consequence, the sand flew upwards and caught the prevailing wind, blew back in this face and covered his body. When the sandstorm died down he was so perfectly camouflaged we could barely see him.

It was at this point that I noticed Lozza had a handkerchief in his mouth and his shoulders were shaking. My eyes were watering with suppressed mirth and I wanted to go to the toilet. The dam broke when the sand-blasted figure in the bunker said, 'And what's so bloody funny?' At least that's what we think he said. It came out as, 'Anwassoblurryunny,' which is how a man speaks with a mouthful of sand.

The trouble with laughing uncontrollably is that from

a distance it seems as if you might have been shot or are having a fit. The team coming up behind told us later that they were gravely concerned to see two of us doubled up and holding our bellies as if being sick while the other member of the team – by this time Michael had seen the funny side of his predicament too – appeared to have collapsed in a writhing heap in the bunker.

In the end, Michael took seven shots to get out of the sand and scored an 11. Six holes later, on the short par three, he hit another bunker.

'Here we go again,' he said. When we got there, the ball had disappeared. We all saw it fall into the bunker but could find no trace of it. It was as if the bunker had opened up and swallowed the ball. We took it as a sign that the gods were not to be abused again. We played quietly to the clubhouse.

Lozza had the best round and, in spite of his troubles, Michael played better than I did, which gives you a fair idea of the kind of morning I had.

Later that day, I watched Señor Ballesteros and the rest show us how the game ought to be played. Of course they did have certain advantages. For instance, no one re-minded Seve on the first tee that he wasn't getting any younger. On the other hand, if he took seven shots to get out of a bunker or played a round of golf like I did, it would be a major disaster rather than a belly laugh.

The price you pay for perfection is the serious nature of the pursuit. Those of us who settle for less have much more fun.

July 1990

Would-be Masters
Now Only Martyrs

I HAVE not played much golf lately. I have not given up, or anything sensible like that. It is simply that I needed time to reassess my relationship with golf, to work out why it is I sometimes play with the rhythm and style of the young Gary Player and other times in the manner of an old and feeble prat.

What I am looking for is a level of mediocrity below which I never fall. The present situation is that there are no boundaries to my incompetence.

The trouble with writing about your misadventures is that they become enshrined in golfing folklore. For instance, the account of the round I played with Messrs Holloway and Barratt on Captain's Day at Temple Golf Club is to be hung in the clubhouse along with our scorecards.

There it will remain, to enable future generations to have a laugh at our incompetence. We have, I suppose, the consolation of immortality, but we would rather be living legends than dead ones.

What people will not understand when they read the

article is that the three of us have had our moments, which we would willingly tell you about except no one would be interested. Nowadays people are only interested in bad news, which is sad because I have played with Michael when he has looked like the best 20 handicapper in the world.

If he can avoid the bunkers and get his putter working he is a formidable opponent. His putter is an extraordinary implement, having a whirl of Technicolor woods on its face. On the odd occasions he gets the head squared up with the hole he puts so sweetly that Messrs Rice and Lloyd-Webber should consider re-uniting to write the musical about it – 'Barratt and The Amazing Technicolor Dreamputter'.

Similarly, I have played with Lozza when his swing was so graceful and fluent it looked like Johnny Hodges sounds. I told him this once but he said he would rather be compared with Ben Webster. He can be a touch pedantic about music.

Nonetheless, there was a time some years ago when, as a humble 17 handicapper, he broke the course record by shooting a gross 76, net 59. No one wrote an article about that; nor was it recorded, until now, that two years ago I stood with Lozza on the eighteenth at Temple needing to sink a tiddly putt to beat his record by one shot. I lipped out and equalled Lozza's performance.

I became a 12 handicap golfer, like Lozza, and things have gone downhill ever since. Even so, I did have that moment of glory when golf seemed the easiest game in the world and I was convinced that if I kept at it I would soon be earning a fortune with Gary, Lee and Chi-Chi on the Seniors' Tour.

I was talking about this very subject with Lozza the other day. He had called round to ask if I kept my card for Captain's Day because they were going to frame it. I had, of course, torn it up on the eleventh, where, with all shots gone, I placed my approach to the green nearer Bisham Abbey than the flag. Nonetheless, I had no problem reliving the horror: I started with a six on a par four and then went 6 (4), 5 (4), 6 (5), 4 (3), 6 (4), 3 (4), 4 (3), 6 (5), 3 (3) and finished on the eleventh with a five-wood towards Marlow via Bisham.

I completed a new card, signed it and handed it to Lozza. As he scrutinised it, I said, 'Do you remember when I equalled your score at Temple?'

'Yes I do,' he said. Then he said, almost to himself, 'He must have been possessed.' I hope they don't make too much fuss about hanging the article and the scorecards. It could have a grievous effect upon my rehabilitation.

Generally speaking people have been very kind. Apart from letters of commiseration, I have received three videos featuring advice by Tom Kite, Seve Ballesteros and Nick Faldo and an anonymous donor sent me a book called *The Inner Game of Golf.* I was also sent a pamphlet listing alternative hobbies for senior citizens such as doing tapestry and making tea cosies. I suspect this came from my friend Jimmy Tarbuck.

To be frank, I have discovered that the only consolation for a bad round of golf is to find someone who is worse off than you are. It is why, on these occasions, I look towards my pal Al. His theory about golf is that it was invented as certain proof that life was not meant to be easy. He believes that the selling of golf as a leisure pursuit is a fraud and that golf bags, particularly those sold to middle-aged golfers, should carry a health warning.

He eschews golf lessons and coaching manuals and puts his faith in technology. At one time or another he has had the entire history of golf engineering in his bag, often all at the same time. He has the biggest and heaviest golf bag I have ever seen. Caddies scatter and feign injury as he approaches the pro's shop. Of those who dare to carry for him only the few trained by the Long Range Desert Group to survive like camels come through the ordeal unscathed.

He took up golf because his doctor suggested it might be a good way to relieve the tensions and frustrations of his job. He now looks forward to work as a relief from golf and the doctor gives him tranquillisers to get him on the course. He is sometimes known as 'Two Gloves Al' because he wears a glove on either hand.

This stops him biting his nails down to the second knuckle during a round. Although he refuses to pay for expert advice, he is willing to listen to anyone with a theory about how to play the game. The other day he met a man in a pub who told him that the perfect posture at address was to imagine he was sitting on a bar stool.

At the same time another customer suggested that he might find it easier hitting the ball if he widened his stance. You don't have to be clever to understand that the two pieces of advice are incompatible. Nonetheless, my pal Al has managed to incorporate them both in his set-up. So if you see a man squatting on a golf course looking like a bandy-legged fellow trying to sit on a tall bar stool, you will have met my pal.

In his unremitting search for sorrow and aggravation on the golf course he has travelled where few have been. The tranquillisers he uses are the kind given to animals to make their trip to the slaughter-house seem a pleasant one and they give his temper in moments of stress a benign malevolence.

Once, after he had seven-putted on a par three after finishing five feet from the pin with his tee shot, he enquired of his caddie, 'Do you know what I would

do if the man who invented golf walked on to this green right now?' The caddie shook his head. 'I would poke his eyes out with my putter,' said Al.

He is much concerned with metaphysical and philosophical issues raised by the game, such as if golf is a metaphor for man's struggle against his environment, why was it necessary to invent bunkers? Another of his concerns is how the man who invents a missile capable of entering a building through a keyhole from a hundred miles away can be the same fellow who misses a two-foot putt.

I have yet to discuss with him the latest theory on the subject of putting. This comes from a sports psychologist who suggests that random recitation can cure the yips. Dr Richard Masters, of York University, says that we should forget teaching manuals and start reciting letters of the alphabet when putting, especially for money. What Al will make of this I do not know.

His current thinking on the subject is that the lining up of the putt is best done from a horizontal position. What he does is flatten himself on the green and sight his putter head behind the ball. The difficult part is getting to his feet while keeping the putter in the correct position. He thinks the solution might be a putter he can use from a kneeling position. What the R & A will make of all this is anybody's guess.

The other day I met one of my great heroes, Gary Player, who asked me about my game. When I told him, he suggested the only way out of my predicament was practice. It was sensible and kindly advice, but not what I wanted to hear. For all I admire Gary Player, my pal Al remains my role model.

The fact is we enjoy our pursuit of mediocrity and I suspect that in the unlikely event of us becoming as good as Mr Player, we would give the game up and find something else to bellyache about.

July 1991

Furtive Golfing Gigglers Entitled to Claim Relief

IT IS NOW an accepted ritual of Captain's Day at Temple Golf Club that the field is led off by Messrs Barratt, Holloway and Parkinson. What started as a jolly wheeze has become a tradition which is all very fine if you are the kind of chap who likes getting up at 5.30 a.m. to be on the first tee at 6.25 having your photograph taken.

At least this year it was sunny and we could see the photographer and vice versa. In recent years the snapper has had to use a flash to find us and the photographs caught us looking bleary and surprised, like criminals in mug shots. In fact I have little doubt that had the local paper published the photographs we would all have been pulled in for questioning by the local constabulary for a variety of unsolved crimes.

On this day it was bright and sunny as we stood on the first tee and surveyed our adventure. The clouds were high and ribbed. Lozza informed us that this was what is known as a buttermilk sky. I said Hoagy Carmichael once wrote a song called 'Ol' Buttermilk Sky'. Lozza said it was Johnny Mercer.

It was no good asking Michael Barratt, whose musical knowledge is contained in the recording careers of Rosemary Clooney and Guy Mitchell. In any case, the problem with having a conversation with Michael on a golf course is that one can never find him. He is always in some inaccessible part of the landscape startling rabbit and pheasant in his search for the ball. He would make an excellent beater for a shoot.

We lost him for the first time on the second hole. For those of you who have not played Temple, the second hole is something you do not need at the start of a medal round. It is a long par four, uphill, into a prevailing wind and, in my view, the toughest hole on the course.

When Lozza and I eventually reached the green and looked around for our friend he was so far away he looked a distant speck. As he came towards us, we were reminded, irresistibly, of that marvellous scene in 'Lawrence of Arabia' when the dot on the horizon becomes Omar Sharif on a camel.

Michael is not a demonstrative man but he was clearly unhappy when he arrived on the green and not a little fatigued after his long journey. He four-putted and finished with a 10.

He asked rhetorically, as golfers do, what was wrong with his putting. We suggested that he might cut a couple of inches from his putter like Nick Faldo. I said that instead of taking it from the shaft of the putter he should cut off the bottom of the club and use what was left like a snooker cue. Not surprisingly, he was not amused.

This raised the complex moral and philosophical argument about whether or not it was right to make fun at the misery of others on a golf course. It came up the other day when I was watching the Kemper Open on Sky Television. The cameras picked out the forlorn figure of one Jeff Wagner, a young pro playing his first major tournament on the American circuit. The reason for singling him out was that as he approached the eighteenth green on his second round he was 30 odd shots over par. He looked like a man having a nightmare.

It didn't help that his cap appeared too big for his head and the face underneath was miserable and hapless. He looked like a sad chipmunk. At the same time there was something risible about his predicament. As he came to the eighteenth, he was nearly 50 shots off the lead.

At any rate he certainly tickled the commentators, because when they tried to describe Wagner's progress down the eighteenth fairway they started giggling and fairly soon were incapable of making any sound other than the infectious noise people make when they grunt and snort with suppressed laughter.

At the time the unfortunate Wagner was hacking his way out of a huge bunker and saying to a fairway camera something along the lines of 'a man's gotta do what a man's gotta do'. I must admit that at this point in proceedings I too was helpless with laughter.

Back in the studio the excellent David Livingstone, who presents the programme, and Peter Oosterhuis were

most definitely not amused. Quite the opposite. They
thought it unfair and unseemly for commentators to
laugh at the misfortune of a golf professional.

Their feeling must have had an echo in America
because the next day, blow me down if we didn't see
Wagner sitting with one of those magisterial American
interviewers, being treated like visiting royalty.

Wagner had become a celebrity. The man who was a
joke the day before had become a star and the more he
told his story – how his life had been a terrible struggle
and being so broke his girlfriend gave him the money to
pay the entrance fee to the competition – the more the
commentators seemed like crass and insensitive oafs.

However, Wagner's sensitive performance did nothing
to dissuade me from the opinion that the commentators
were quite right to have a laugh at his expense, and that
in my view not enough of it goes on. We are all in danger
of taking sport too seriously and it is a malaise that
spreads from the top downwards.

Perhaps if we started taking more mickey out of our
sporting heroes it might persuade all of us to loosen up a
bit and treat a game as a recreational pastime and not a
matter of life and death.

It is one thing believing this and quite another trying to
persuade your friend who has just made 10 on a par four
that his day has not been completely ruined.

So Lozza and I decided we would be more sympathetic
to Michael's predicament. In any case we were having a
lousy time ourselves, playing such awful golf that we
both took 50 shots to play the front nine.

Our play improved on the back nine; Michael's didn't. His predicament became so grotesque that I could feel our hysteria mounting as mishap piled on mishap and his score increased. The dam of suppressed mirth nearly burst as we walked up the seventeenth fairway when, after a scuffed drive, Michael enquired, plaintively, what he was doing wrong.

At that moment he had taken 106 shots in his round so we assumed his question was again of the rhetorical variety. I presume that was why Lozza didn't answer. In truth I dared not look at him in case a glance triggered a bout of hysterics.

Our resolve finally cracked on the eighteenth tee. Michael's drive was a low hooking shot with enough curve to strike Lozza's golf bag, which was parked at mid wicket. What Lozza keeps in his bag is his own business, but it was of sufficient resilience to launch the ball back towards the tee. We ducked as it whistled over our heads and disappeared into the long grass. It was the most amazing rebound I have ever witnessed.

As we cowered on the tee like men sheltering from a mortar attack, Michael began bollocking Lozza for parking his trolley in front of his drive. This was too much. Like the American commentators we had reached the point where laughter was a merciful release. You would have thought as you saw us walk happily up the fairway that we were having the time of our lives. And of course we were.

We had walked five miles or so through beech and cherry, oak and pine, on a sunny day under a buttermilk sky. And even though Michael had compiled a score that Brian Lara would be proud of, he could tell his children that for one moment in time he was the third on the leaderboard in the clubhouse.

We'll come back for more punishment next year, God willing. And I still think it was Hoagy Carmichael who write 'Ol' Buttermilk Sky'. If so, it was the only thing I got right all day.

June 1994

A Man in a Bunker is a Continuous Hoot

N EVER mind the Open. The big story in golf was at Temple Golf Club. Captain's Day brought together the members in a heart-warming display of British manhood. They ranged from callow youth to grizzled veteran, persimmon drivers to Big Berthas, those who play with a testosterone vigour and those awaiting the arrival of the golfing equivalent of Viagra.

I am not revealing any secrets when I say that our threeball belongs to the latter category. No longer mighty off the tee, we place our faith in medical science and play a waiting game. Since I started writing about the adventures of our threeball, private grief has become public anguish.

Michael Barratt, hitherto best remembered as a splendidly acerbic television interviewer, is now celebrated as 'Bunker' Barratt because of the time he has spent in the sand during past Captain's Days. Similarly, Lozza Holloway, the piano player, spent enough time in a bunker on the fifth a couple of years ago to be rechristened 'Hanson' Holloway after John Hanson who was renowned for his rendition of 'The Desert Song'.

A Man in a Bunker is a Continuous Hoot

I have a reputation as a smart-ass and a snitch because of my accounts of our games, which critics suspect are angled to make fun of my playing partners while ignoring my own deficiencies. Maybe this article will answer those accusations. I have a tale to tell so poignant and sad it may move you to tears. On the other hand it may not, in which case I can only assume you are made of stone or know nothing of the trauma suffered by mug golfers.

By comparison to the rest of us, the pros have it easy. They ought to be good at the game. They have nothing else to do all day but practise. What about the rest of us who have to fit golf into a busy routine? When was the last time Nick Faldo walked round a golf course worrying about his chip shop going out of business or trying to fit in eighteen holes before, during or after a day at the office? When was the last time he had to worry about buying a set of golf clubs, or practising with concrete balls or raking bunkers?

The reality of golf, the real drama and romance of the game, is to be found in the aspirations of club golfers. I decided to approach Captain's Day like a pro. In fact I went to see one. He said it might be a good idea to video my swing. I had always resisted the temptation, having in my mind's eye, the image of a simple but classic action with little room for improvement. What I saw changed my life. There was this hunched, tense figure gripping the club like a sledgehammer with what could best be described as a grudging swing.

If the image I had of my action was free flowing, the reality was constipated. My pro was skilled and caring and suggested one or two remedies. But the damage had been done. I now saw myself as others did: more Tommy Cooper than Tommy Horton.

It was in this depressed state of mind that I stood on the first tee at Temple. It was 6.30 on a grey morning and there was a faint mist over distant Marlow. So far as we could tell. In fact, what is normally an uninterrupted view to the far horizon was in danger of being obscured by the height of the grass in the rough.

There was little doubt that a misguided ball would be discovered only after an inch-by-inch search by a line of specially trained policemen, or, alternatively, a combine harvester.

I had a bet with Lozza about how long it would be before our partner would ask, 'What am I doing wrong?' It is a question he asks every Captain's Day and so far we have not managed a satisfactory answer.

As a matter of fact we had to wait until we had played the third hole. By this time Michael had 27 on the card. Perhaps a more delicate way of putting it is to say he was 15 over fours. On the other hand his sequence of scores was 10, 9 and 8 so you could argue he was getting better. Lozza was steady and I was chugging along until we came to the sixth. To set the scene: this is the hole between the fifth (Lozza's nemesis two years ago) and the seventh (re-christened Barratt's Bunker).

It is a 370 yard par four and straightforward. I put my second shot into the greenside bunker, which was my first mistake. My second was trying to get it out. What I should have done is feigned illness, or pretended I had left the gas on at home, or taken a shovel instead of a sand iron. As it was I hit my first bunker shot into the face of the hazard, the second into my own footprints and the third excavated about a ton of the chalk upon which Temple is built. It was at this point I became aware that my playing partners were trying hard not to laugh.

What every golfer knows is that in spite of (or perhaps because of) the good manners of the game, it is impossible not to be amused by the travails of a man in a bunker. There is no more humiliating, revealing and risible situation in the whole of sport. A batsman being tonked in the box comes close.

But that is a one-off joke. A man in a bunker is a continuous hoot, a never ending boffo. Every failed shot is a repetition of the punch line. The laughter develops in direct reaction to the victim's increasing discomfort. Suffice to say I took seven shots to get on to the green by which time my partners were in danger of wetting themselves. I three-putted to card a 12. When he had finished laughing Michael said he looked forward to reading my account in the *Telegraph*. He added he was glad he wasn't the only one playing like a pillock.

The rest of the round was played to the beat of a muffled drum. I went round in 92 (net 78). Michael stopped counting after safely reaching his century, but Lozza shot 78 (net 65). He won the Veterans' Shield and had a chance for the tournament but was unable to play the second round in the afternoon. He had to travel to London to play piano at a Royal Gala Concert. A true all-rounder.

And that's another thing. When was the last time Colin Montgomerie played a round of golf while rehearsing a Gershwin medley. Spoiled is what they are. Don't know they're born. More importantly, they don't know what they are missing.

July 1998

Struggling with my Inability to Conquer a Frivolous Pastime

I F ONLY took a minute. Two swings of my seven-iron, to be precise. Then Mr Alan Barber, of Windlesham, asked me to accompany him to his office, where he showed me the video. As I took the club back my front knee instead of moving behind the ball shot forward like an England batsman playing Muralitharan. Most remarkable. At the peak of my swing, I was bow-legged. At the moment I ought to have been coiled to strike, my legs formed an aperture through which could be driven a decent-sized family car.

'The only wonder is how you hit the ball at all, never mind badly,' said Mr Barber. I asked him if he had ever seen anything like it. He is a polite and diplomatic fellow but, even so, had to admit what I had done was pretty strange.

I rang up Lozza Holloway, my playing partner, and asked him why he hadn't said anything.

'About what?' he said.

'What's wrong with my swing,' I said.

'I never look,' he said.

'Why not?' I asked, a bit miffed.

'I daren't,' he said. Charming.

I asked Mr Bellow, with whom I had spent three days golfing in Ireland. Hadn't he noticed my front knee shooting forward? He said he hadn't but then he could never work out left-handers because they always had their backs to their partners on the tee. Yet another example of the way we are discriminated against.

Anyway, Mr Barber took me out to the practice range and within a couple of minutes I was hitting the ball solidly and straight. It is a strange game. One minute you are in the bunker of despond, next minute life is a gimme putt. In a twinkling, Mr Barber had reduced my mountain of despair to a foothill of hope. I was thinking of adopting him. I promised I would practise but of course I didn't.

The reason there are so many golf pros around the place and why they are so busy is because most golfers who seek their advice think that is all they have to do. They regard a visit to the pro as being the equivalent of absolution. In other words, once they have been told what they are doing wrong, the problem is solved. All they have to do to win the monthly medal is turn up. When it doesn't work, we find another golf pro.

Not that I am thinking of leaving Mr Barber. He keeps things simple and businesslike, unlike some I could mention. I had lessons from one golf pro who talked incessantly about himself for fifteen minutes and when we finally got down to business, he hit more balls than I did. Another was so technical he might as well have conducted the entire session in Urdu, for all I understood what was going on.

A week after my lesson, I stood on the first tee at Sunningdale, certain the worst was behind me. Mr Barber had provided me with the key to future happiness. I spanked the ball down the fairway of the first on the Old Course. My caddie, who had seen me play before, nearly fell over with shock. It didn't last long. On the next hole I deliberately drew back my knee in the approved fashion, then hit the ball over deep extra cover into the woods. It didn't swerve. It went straight in as if aimed in that direction. Similarly at the next hole and so it went on. There was the occasional indication I had played the game before. I drove the green on the short ninth and won a shirt by getting nearest the pin on the par-three thirteenth.

But generally, I played like my Auntie Nellie. Back in the clubhouse, I went to have my swing analysed by a pro who had videoed all the participants.

'What's this?' he asked, pointing at the screen and indicating my knee. I told him my swing thought was to get it past the ball, as instructed by Mr Barber, of Windlesham.

'Mr Barber was quite right but he didn't tell you to move your body as well, did he?' he said. And he stopped the tape at the top of my swing so I could clearly see I had swayed off the ball.

A fault begets a correction begets another fault begets a

lesson and so on, until eventually I throw myself in front of a fast-moving golf buggy. My golfing misery is never ending. It occurs to me there is another world golfers visit which is closed to me. This is where players 'rip it' or are described as being 'on fire'. They operate in some kind of mystical trance, a condition known as 'being in the zone'. They are forever 'focused'. I know not of what they speak. I struggle within the boundaries of my own incompetence, focused only on my own inability to conquer a frivolous pastime.

I suspect Mrs Parkinson spends a lot of time 'in the zone'; more than is good for her, I shouldn't wonder. We are off to Australia soon so I asked her to make a list of things we might need on the trip. Top of the list was the heading 'Swing Thought For Oz', followed by 'Left shoulder under chin, swish through ball'.

My swing thought is not to take the golf clubs. It is the only way I will return feeling better than when I left. Cold turkey. I'll let you know how long it lasts.

October 1998